The *Write* Book
for Christian Families

Robert Allen

 Bob Jones University Press
Greenville, South Carolina 29614

Library of Congress Cataloging-in-Publication Data

Allen, Robert A., 1946-
    The write book for Christian families / Robert Allen.
      p.   cm.
    Includes index.
    ISBN 0-89084-723-1
    1. Christian literature—Authorship. 2. Family—Religious life. 3. Christian educa-
tion—Home training. 4. Christian education of children. 5. Children—Religious life.
I. Title.
BR117.A44   1993
808'.0662—dc20   93-37031
                                                  CIP

The Write Book for Christian Families

Robert Allen

Edited by Greg Kuzmic
Designed by Doug Young
Cover designed by Matthew Donovan

© 1993 Bob Jones University Press
Greenville, South Carolina 29614

ISBN 0-89084-723-1

15   14   13   12   11   10   9   8   7   6   5   4   3   2

Contents

Dedication

To Christopher Robert Allen who came along too late to be a part of the Bible Story Family programs, but who will benefit from everything his mother and I learned while raising his older brothers and sisters to write and serve God.

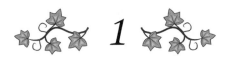

The Write Track

Family adventures are usually described in terms of two-week canoe trips through the Boundary Waters Canoe Area, an extended visit to Disney World, or camping in the Black Hills. Thousands of dollars invested in computer games and hundreds of hours in front of the television set are considered normal activities for many families. This book offers an alternative that can become the greatest adventure for God your family has ever encountered: family writing!

These suggestions will also help your family get started on writing that can be a means of serving God. Don't think of this as a textbook but as a choose-your-own-adventure book. Read it carefully, then make use of the hints that sound right for you and for your children at their present ages.

Maybe you have never been a writer yourself. You find it a chore even to write letters; you would rather pay for a long-distance telephone call. Perhaps you had an English teacher who rapped you on the knuckles when you failed to write complete sentences. Don't worry. This is a book of family fun, and no one is going to check your papers for correct grammar or punctuation. Your family will enjoy themselves and be more creative if you don't check their writing either.

One of our family's greatest adventures involved a weekly trip to the radio station in the Virginia town where we lived. Every Saturday morning we had our own fifteen-minute program called "The Bible Story Family." Kent and Tammy were not yet in school, so my wife, Carmen, helped them to memorize their lines earlier in the week. Then we practiced with Chad and Wendy after school to make sure we were ready for our taping session.

"This is Chad, Wendy, Kent, and Tammy, with their parents," the announcer would say, "and they have two more exciting stories for you today. So put your listening ears on, boys and girls, and get ready for 'The Bible Story Family' with the Allens."

Being on radio provided a family adventure that we looked forward to every week instead of just once a year at vacation time. It was fun to hear your voice on the radio each Saturday morning after you'd made a tape earlier in the week. It was a thrill to sit at a microphone and have a real announcer give you the cue to start reading. But best of all, it was exciting to serve God together as a family.

One of our greatest concerns as parents has been to communicate to our children a desire to serve God. Not that we thought they had to become pastors, missionaries, or teachers. We've never liked the concept that only certain full-time careers qualify as Christian service. The entire Christian life is a life of service to God. We have found it to be an adventure, and we wanted to communicate that sense of excitement to our children.

Since our own parents had managed to raise us in parsonages without alienating us from the ministry, we asked ourselves what they had done. The answer was quite simple. They had involved us in their ministries. My father, a church-planting missionary in the western states, had me lead singing for him when I was still too short to see over the pulpit. He solved that problem by putting me up on a chair. My wife's parents ate oatmeal for lunch in order to save enough money to buy musical instruments for their seven children. Working out the answer in the lives of our own children has been a lifelong effort, just as it was for them. Encouraging our children to write has been a vital part of that effort.

One teacher tells of a first grader named Alicia whose mother took her and three other children to the museum every Saturday morning. When Alicia wrote about those experiences for school, her mother would tell her that her writing was beautiful. Simply by listening and asking questions and exclaiming over Alicia's writing, she taught her daughter to make writing a natural part of her day-to-day activities.

"The need for children to learn to communicate through writing has never been greater," says Dorothy Rich in *MegaSkills* (Boston: Houghton Mifflin Co., 1988). "In the past, there was more dependence on oral communication. Today, you have to be able to put words on paper."

Children won't start by writing books and sermons and hymns. They will start by scribbling captions over pictures in magazines, carrying on long conversations with mythical friends, and making signs for their doll houses and train layouts. But they are writing.

The important thing is not what children write, but simply that they write. They may write recipes, letters, skits, stories, bulletin copy, television scripts, jokes, Bible commentaries, poems, songs, pageants, computer programs, cartoon strips, Christmas programs, plays, books, and even thank-you notes, and have fun doing it. At the same time, they will be creating an invaluable family heirloom, a treasure that will preserve memories, entertain grandparents, create family unity and provide a basis for educational success.

In later years, you might receive an invitation, as I recently did from Wendy, who has been writing since her childhood and is now almost grown-up.

"Dad, would you come into the living room? I have something to show you."

I pushed my chair back from the supper table and followed Wendy to the front room.

"There, on the piano."

Sitting down at my wife's Kawai, I began to pick out the chords on the piece of manuscript paper in front of me. As I played, Wendy started to sing.

At the times in your life
when nothing seems to go your way,
Look to Jesus, He will guide you
and give you strength for every day.
Every day the Lord is there beside you.
Every day His Word is there unchanged and true.
He'll never leave you even though you might stray,
But draw you back to His perfect way.

No radio announcer will play that song on your gospel radio station next week, but to me it was one of the most beautiful songs I had ever heard. Wendy had written it: every word of the lyrics, every measure of the music. It was a creation, uniquely her own.

The same summer, Chad, our oldest son, wrote to us from High Point Camp in Pennsylvania where he was working. The letter began with a long poem detailing what had happened since he had arrived a week earlier.

After the poem he continued, "I will be working here as a lifeguard and counselor and skit director and a couple of other duties without titles. I am in the process of completing a five-day progressive skit. We are trying to organize a drama team here to teach the kids basic acting skills. It should be a lot of fun."

Writing—a lot of fun? It can be for your family. But it can also be a means of serving God.

Educators experienced in teaching children to write remind us that children who lack opportunities to exercise their imaginations and express themselves creatively often find that imaginative and free use of language becomes increasingly difficult as they grow older.

Writing to serve others will become easier if it is practiced from an early age. Get your family started on the write track.

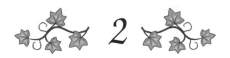

The Write Path

The thrilling moment has arrived: your child's graduation from the church nursery. For the next fifteen years, with time out for broken arms, colds, and the flu bug, your children will probably join you in the "big" service. What do you do with a two-minute attention span during a thirty-minute message? Some parents pack a survival kit of books, games, and toys. Others scowl as children develop their own entertainment, like counting all the holes in the acoustic tile on the ceiling of the auditorium, or counting all the songs in the hymnbook with one-word titles.

Some children (and adults) sleep. One pastor admitted that he counted more than twenty-five parishioners asleep during a morning service. He attributed it to the lack of air conditioning on a warm summer day.

Write a Sermon Notebook

Why not try the "write" path for involvement in church services on the child's own age level—a sermon notebook. It will provide mental and physical activity for your child and will aid him in learning how to listen to the Word of God.

Construct a sermon notebook for each child by stapling together several sheets of paper. Make them of a size that will fit easily inside the cover of a Bible. Then put them with your Bible and reserve them for use during church. Only one rule is necessary: The child must write or draw something in the notebook that is related to the sermon.

Since children love to imitate adults, this project will be more effective if parents are also taking notes on the sermon. Your children will see that you consider it important to make an effort to remember what is being shared from the Word of God. What is important to you will also become important to them.

For the younger child, one scribbled word or perhaps a drawing may be all that is produced during a service. After hearing a message on "The Judgment Seat of Christ," Wendy came home with a picture of herself on the witness stand complete with a halo. Around her were dozens of stick-figure people observing her testimony. It was a visual summary of the message, evidence that she had been listening.

Sometimes our children's notebooks contained a paragraph, like the one on Dorcas. Wendy wrote: "Dorcas is a woman who believed in God. She gave to those around her, her death was prepared for nicely. Jesus raised her and she was blessed."

Many times we learned important lessons from what the children put in their sermon notebooks. Kent heard James and John called the "sons of thunder" during a sermon and decided that if there were "sons" of thunder, their father had to be a big thunder. What an application to those who are raising children! Our children will be just like us.

It isn't always the message that makes the greatest impression on children. Sermon notebooks may contain prayer lists, announcements, or the titles of songs that were sung. Not until our children were into their early teens did we see fledgling outlines appear. But that was fine. They were learning on their own level. Regardless of what they write, praise them for listening and putting down their impressions.

Write for the Family Altar

Any family that attempts to be consistent in a daily family devotional time discovers quickly how much variety is necessary. Writing can provide that variety. The ideas that follow may be easily adapted to any age. Choose the ones that appeal to your family right now and save the others for a later time.

Give a Reason

As you read a portion from the Scriptures, have each person write down one verse reference. Then they should write down a reason they chose that verse. The reasons should be personal. Too often children are required to repeat what they think adults want to hear. One child might choose a verse because it has a new word that is fun to say, like "sluggard" (Prov. 20:4). Another may find that the verse "A merry heart maketh a cheerful countenance" (Prov. 15:13) reminds her of a joke: "Why did the chicken cross to the middle of the road? Because she wanted to lay it on the line."

Don't correct the reasons or try to make them all theological truths. The important thing is that children are listening to the Word of God and relating it to something that is personal to them.

Use Group Story Writing

Start a story by writing one sentence at the top of a sheet of paper. Then pass the paper around and have everyone add a sentence to the first one. This process may continue as long as ideas are flowing freely. When the story has concluded, have someone read it aloud.

Starting with a familiar Bible character will help children participate because they will be able to share information from past experience. "David checked his pouch to make sure the stones he had picked up from the brook were still there" would lead easily to a step-by-step encounter with Goliath.

Starting with a contemporary situation will help them consider solutions to predicaments they may be facing. "Billy grabbed the crayon away from Andy and screamed, 'It's my turn! You've been coloring all morning.' "

Don't use your own children's names. It will be much more fun if they can write about other children who, just incidentally, act a lot like they do.

Caption Pictures

Find pictures that relate in some fashion to the portion of Scripture you are presently studying as a family. These can be pictures of biblical events from Bible-story books or simply pictures from magazines. Have each person write a short caption for the picture and then share it. For a picture of Noah's ark you might get "A real moving experience" or "The two-by-two zoo."

Create Cartoon Conversations

Using the same pictures as in the previous exercise, have each person create his own cartoon. Cut circles out of blank paper and tape them above the heads of the people or animals in the picture. Then, inside the circles, write the conversation that might be taking place between the characters in the picture.

The conversations may be factual. A picture of Jesus holding children on His lap could have Jesus saying, "Bring the children to me," while the children say, "Hi, Jesus." That would show an understanding of Christ's love for, and acceptance of, the children.

The conversations may also be fictional. Paul, being lowered over the wall in a basket, might say, "Here I come, ready or not."

It's not exactly scriptural, but it captures the excitement that was definitely a part of that incident in his life.

Another variation of this activity is to give each person a sheet of paper and have him write an entire paragraph or story based on what he sees in the picture. This will take longer, but it can furnish real enjoyment when the stories are read. Collect all the writings in a loose-leaf binder, and they will be a great delight to your children five or ten years later.

Connect Words

When the family is studying a particular Bible story, write key words on slips of paper and have each person take five of them at random. Using those five words, they should write a single sentence that includes all of them. If the family has been reading Acts 16, someone might get the words "prison," "marketplace," "Jesus," "earthquake," and "Lydia." He could write, "Paul went to prison because he talked about Jesus in the marketplace, and an earthquake destroyed the prison so he could go back to Lydia's house."

Expand a Word

Write a single word, such as "sword," at the top of a page. Pass the paper around and have everyone write down something about a sword. You might get "a sword is sharp," and "a sword is for fighting." But as the list gets longer, you may also come up with "the Word of God is like a sword" or "David used Goliath's sword to defeat him." Continue to write as long as the ideas come easily.

Make Up a Play

Children enjoy acting. One of the favorite devotional activities of our children was the chance to act out Bible stories and see whether the rest of the family could guess which story it was. These skits were often performed in pantomime. Wendy would ride into the living room on Chad's back, and we knew it was Mary going to Egypt on the donkey. Tamara would kneel to pray while Kent opened his mouth in a silent roar, and we knew Daniel was in the lion's den.

Adding words to Bible skits can also be a lot of fun. A good place to start is with the monologue. The key to writing a good monologue is to have a silent listener. Ask "What would Daniel have said to those lions when he was thrown into the den with them?" Then have your child write the answer, using the words he might use if he were Daniel. "Boy, I sure hope you fellows aren't hungry. I'm not very tasty, you know, just skin and bones. Now, my sister, there's a real meal for you."

Samson could tell his story to the boy who led him to the pillars of the Philistine temple just before he died. Or David could tell his mother about his adventure with Goliath. Josiah's discovery of the book of God in the temple could be recounted to his best friend. Tell your young writer to imagine that listener while he is writing the monologue, and it will be like telling his best friend something that happened to him.

Writing original dialogue is also a good way to bring Bible stories to life. Start with two characters, like Cain and Abel, and have someone write out the conversation that might have taken place between them just before Cain killed his brother. Or divide your family into pairs and have one person write one side of the conversation and the other one write the other side.

> Abel: You knew you were supposed to bring a lamb for an offering, Cain.
> Cain: How was I supposed to know that?
> Abel: God told our father, and he told us.
> Cain: You're just saying that because you raise sheep.
> Abel: No, that's what God said to do.
> Cain: Well, I wanted to bring fruit, so there.

Adam and Eve, Miriam and the pharaoh's daughter, Abraham and Isaac, Ruth and Boaz, David and Jonathan, Saul and the witch of Endor, Jonah and the big fish, and many other pairs in Scripture are good candidates for dialogue writing. The vocabulary may change as your children grow, but the exercise of actually putting words into the mouths of Bible characters will make them seem real, no matter what the age of the child.

Conduct Interviews

Another variation of the dialogue is to conduct an interview with a Bible character. Write out the questions you would like to ask him and then have someone else write out the answers or simply give them orally. This activity will work well if you have the children write out the questions and the adults answer them, trying to stay as close as possible to the answers the Bible characters would really give.

This method of sharing history can be very effective, as illustrated by the actors who sometimes portray soldiers at Appomattox Court House, Virginia. No matter what question is asked concerning themselves or the events of the Civil War, they answer the same way a soldier would have answered on that day in history, over 125 years ago.

You may discover that with a little practice your interviewers will become adept at writing tough questions for you to answer, but the facts you will learn about Scripture will make it valuable for both you and them.

Write a Family Bible Commentary

Writing your own Bible commentary is a major project that can provide an extended adventure in Bible study for your family. We did it during a summer when school projects were not demanding great amounts of time. It is an excellent means of learning the Word of God in a family setting and at the same time serving God by helping others to learn.

Start your commentary by choosing a book of the Bible to study. One of the shorter epistles—Philippians, Colossians, Titus, or one of the letters to the Thessalonians—is a good choice.

Gather the necessary study tools and be sure that everyone knows how to use them. A Bible dictionary, a Bible handbook, a concordance, an atlas, and a book on Bible customs should form the core of your research library. Be ready to spend time with younger children so you can teach them how to use these tools.

Next, provide a hardcover three-ring binder in which you will keep the commentary as it is written. Have someone design a cover, perhaps with a family crest on it. You could even have a design contest to see who could come up with the best idea for decorating the cover of your book.

Every day each member of the family should receive an assignment. These can be adjusted to the various age levels, but everyone should feel that he is contributing to the development of the commentary in a significant way. Assignments can be typed or written in longhand. The book will probably be a greater treasure if it preserves copies of the handwriting of each member of the family. Write out each assignment on a separate piece of paper or leave enough room below each question so the answer can be written there. Always keep the questions and answers on the same sheet of paper.

The next day ask the family members to share the results of those assignments, and this will become the family devotional time; then give a new assignment.

Our family chose the book of Philippians. The first assignments grew out of the fact that we discovered the name "Paul" in the first verse.

1. Who wrote the book of Philippians?
2. To whom was the book of Philippians written?
3. When was the book of Philippians written?
4. Where was the book of Philippians written?

The first set of answers should provide an introduction or background to the book. This will involve a comparison with other places in Scripture that mention the characters and places in the book you are studying.

5. Where in the Bible are we told how the church in Philippi began?
6. Who was the first person to be saved in Philippi?

7. Who was the next person saved in Philippi?
8. Who was with Paul when he visited Philippi?
9. Where did they attend prayer meeting?

The background questions should also introduce you to the geography of the book. Include questions that will be answered from an atlas so the family will become acquainted with the location of the events that are taking place.

10. In what country is Philippi located?
11. How far is it from Philippi to Rome?
12. How far is it from Philippi to Jerusalem?

After a general introduction to the book that covers places, times, and circumstances of writing, you will want to focus on the background of the writer. In the case of Philippians, that is Paul. Since many of the introductory questions were also related to him, several facts will already be evident. This is a good time for a personal viewpoint essay. Provide an open-ended sentence for each family member to complete: "I like Paul because . . . ."

Kent, who was going into fifth grade the summer we studied Philippians, wrote the following essay:

I like Paul because he was a very brave preacher and he preached to lots of people and went to lots of places and lots of people got saved from hearing him preach. He was faithful even when the Romans put him and Silas in prison and the philipen jailer got saved.

Tammy, who was going into the third grade that summer, wrote this essay:

> I like Paul because he was very brave and preached the gospel even though some people tried to kill him and he preached and preached and preached and lots of people were saved. One of them was Lydia and she told people about Jesus and Paul preached about Jesus and got thrown into jail and the Philipian jailer got saved.

After completing your introductory materials you are ready to start on a verse-by-verse study of the book. Variety is the key to keeping the project exciting over an extended period of time. Use a mixture of objective and subjective questions.

1. Make a list of every verse in the book where the word "grace" appears.
2. What do you think are the "fruits of righteousness" Paul was talking about in chapter 1, verse 11?

For some of the verses, use the "Explanation, Illustration, Application" approach.

3. What do the words "murmuring" and "disputing" mean in chapter 2, verse 14?
4. Write a sentence you have heard in the past week that could be described as "murmuring."
5. Complete the following sentence: When Tim and Andy get into a fight they should . . . .

Ask older family members to draw maps of the various geographic locations that are mentioned.

6. Draw a map of the Mediterranean area and locate Macedonia (Phil. 4:15) and Thessalonica (Phil. 4:16) on it.

Other family members could write short stories or biographical sketches about the people who are mentioned. Break up the assignment among several people or spread it out over several days.

7. List all the verses in the Bible where Epaphroditus (Phil. 4:18) is mentioned.
8. Make a list of all the places Epaphroditus lived.
9. Complete the following sentence: I think Paul liked Epaphroditus because . . . .

Provide older family members with questions that will require them to draw conclusions from what they are learning.

10. What do you think is the theme of the book of Philippians?
11. How is it possible to obey the command of Philippians 4:4 to "rejoice in the Lord alway"?

When you have completed your project, take several evenings to sit down and read it aloud. You will be amazed at the insights you as a family have gained through a close study of one book of the Bible.

Write Personal Devotions

Many devotional books available for children emphasize the stories of the Bible, communicating facts concerning Bible times and people. Others take Bible principles and apply them to daily life by means of storytelling. Both of these approaches are good. But often these approaches fall short of actually involving children in a study of the Word of God for themselves. Everything they receive has been sifted through someone else's experiences.

Writing as a part of personal devotions will help a person pay closer attention to what he is reading. It will make him more precise in his evaluation of what he is reading. It will also provide him with a record of his personal growth in Christ through Bible study.

One seventh grader who was interested in music determined to read through the entire Bible and write down every verse that contained a reference to singing or to musical instruments. Over the course of a year he kept a list in his Bible, and by the time the year was over his list was complete.

Another teen-ager filled a small file box with cards that contained personal reactions to the verses he had read in his devotions. At summer camp that teen shared with a counselor the fact that he had read through the Bible once for each year of his age: sixteen times. Writing kept the reading of the Scripture vital to him.

There are many types of writing that can be done as a part of personal devotions. One college professor suggested writing down a command to obey and a promise to enjoy out of each passage that is read. Many of the ideas we shared in the section on writing a family commentary can also be used in personal devotions. Here are some other ideas that have proved useful.

Make Lists

Make one list at a time on a certain topic, or start several lists and add to all of them as Scripture is read each day. Here are some topics to get you started.

1. a list of verses that will help overcome depression
2. all the verses that you could use to help lead a soul to Christ
3. every reference to Peter in the book of Acts
4. all the Old Testament passages quoted in the book of Hebrews
5. verses that talk about writing
6. a list of verses that would offer encouragement to those who have suffered loss

Some of this information is available to you in a concordance. But there is something about compiling your own list that helps you remember and use the information you have accumulated.

Compose Poetry

If your child has a flair for poetry, suggest that he try paraphrasing his devotions in a poetic style. The Psalms are particularly suited to this exercise. One young person worked his way through many of the psalms, writing a poem based on each one. It was not great poetry, certainly not something suitable for publication, but it was of great personal benefit. Paraphrasing Scripture into poetry will demand an understanding of the theme and mood of the psalmist, and it will allow for the expression of the same emotions by the poet. It will make the Scripture personal in a very practical way.

Write Out Prayers

The study of Scripture should be a time of intimate communication with God. As He speaks to your children through the Word, they will want to communicate with Him as well. Writing prayers will aid in concentration during that important aspect of devotions. Your child will become more precise in his approach to God when he is required to make a choice in the words that he uses. As a parent, you may also discover that you will become more honest with God when you require yourself to write what you feel.

Another result of writing out prayers is an increased awareness of repetition. Our children often grow accustomed to repeating the same prayers over and over again. But if we encourage them to write those prayers down and they start writing the same prayer on the next page, they will realize what is happening. Hopefully, such a reminder will help your children to explore additional avenues in their communication with God.

These written prayers are not to be shared with other people. Children should be assured that no one will be reading through their prayer letters to God. Even though written down, they are still prayers to Him, and Him alone.

Write Personal Experiences

Many times the Scripture that is read on a certain day fills a particular need in the life of the reader during that day. Recording these specific incidents will reinforce your conviction that the "word is a lamp unto my feet, and a light unto my path" (Ps. 119:105).

17

As your children write these experiences, encourage them to use all their senses. Ask them to try to recall what they saw and heard, what they touched, and what touched them. Use words that describe what was smelled and what was tasted. These descriptive words will help to make the event vivid in their own minds.

Next, help them draw the spiritual lesson through its scriptural parallel. Ask, "Have you ever felt bitterness, like Naomi when she lost her husband and two sons in Moab?" "Have you ever recognized the voice of God from an unexpected source, like when the donkey spoke to Balaam?" "Has our family ever been drawn closer together, like Abraham and Isaac after their experience on Mt. Moriah?"

Writing down exactly how an experience was affected because of a personal relationship with God through His Word will make the Bible come alive for your children. Experiencing the practical benefits of Bible study will transform their devotional time from a chore to an anticipated activity. As a further benefit, you may discover that it does the same for you.

Continuing this practice over a period of time will provide family members with an invaluable record of how God is working in them "both to will and to do of his good pleasure" (Phil. 2:13).

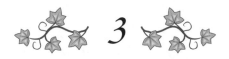

3

Write Away

"The Mystery of the Moose on the Wall" was not a school assignment; it was something Wendy wrote for her own enjoyment and ours as well. Many schools have excellent programs that teach children to write correctly. But there are also ways that you as a family can encourage one another to write and to enjoy writing without waiting for it to be assigned. This chapter will share with you some ways to encourage family members to write, "write away," whatever their ages might be.

The Mystery of the Moose
on the Wall

One bright sunny day in June, Susie, Mary, and Johny were playing hide and go seek. Johny was "it". Susie ran under the table to hide, while Mary ran into the closet.

All of a sudden Susie screamed. Johny and Mary came running. "What's the matter? What's the matter?" they cried.

"I saw the moose on the wall move," she cried. As she pointed to the picture of a moose hanging on the wall. "Don't be silly," said Mary. "You know pictures don't move unless someone pushes them." "Mary's right," said Johny.

That night when everyone was asleep Susie heard something. Then she saw the moose standing in her room! Then she saw him walk over to her and this is what he said, Susie, please don't be afraid of me, please, will you every night feed me some grass? I will be your freind if you do. So Susie cut a hole in the window, but kept the glass, and every night she would take out the glass and get some grass for the moose.

by Wendy, age 8

Build a Writing Climate

Read to Write

Elizabeth Yates in *Someday You'll Write* (New York: E. P. Dutton, 1962) points out that learning to write should start with a child's reading. She suggests that as children read, they be asked why they enjoy that particular book. "If you can begin to discover some of the reasons, you will be laying a solid foundation for your own approach to writing," she concludes.

It is certainly true that writers are readers. Provide your children with the best in literature. Read to them and with them. Have family reading times where you read aloud or when you all sit together in the same room reading to yourselves. Small children like books if their parents enjoy books. They will also enjoy writing if they see that their parents enjoy writing. "Have children see you writing notes to friends, letters to business firms, perhaps stories to share with the children," advises the National Council of Teachers of English. "From time to time, read aloud what you have written and ask your children their opinion of what you've said. If it's not perfect, so much the better. Making changes in what you write confirms for the child that revision is a natural part of writing—which it is."

Develop a Taste for Words

This is another suggestion from the National Council of Teachers of English in its pamphlet "How to Help Your Child Become a Better Writer." As you travel, talk about what you see, hear, smell, taste, and touch. "The basis of good writing is good talk, and younger children especially grow into stronger control of language when loving adults—particularly parents—share experiences and rich talk about those experiences," says the pamphlet.

One excellent place for conversation is the dinner table. Such conversations don't need to be highly structured; that is, you don't have to announce a topic such as "World Trade" and require everyone to say what he thinks. But free-wheeling discussions of current events topics, theology, and what the family plans to do during a coming vacation will get everyone involved.

Share accounts of what happened during the day at work and at school. If Mom and Dad set the pattern of sharing the events of their day, the rest of the family will do the same. Humorous stories or jokes will help the family become aware of language because humor is almost always based upon word choice and arrangement. Even the much-maligned pun is a valuable tool in developing an ear for language. Most children will develop an ear for riddles at about age six. Don't just endure the stage, encourage it. They are learning that similar words can have different meanings.

21

For nearly a year we found it impossible to get through a meal without hearing Kent's favorite joke, "What stands behind a star?" The reason he found such great enjoyment in that joke was that no one ever got the answer right. If they said, "A policeman," which had been the original answer when he first learned the joke, he would giggle and say, "No, another star." If we tried, "Another star" as an alternative answer, he would revert to "A policeman," thrilled that he had pulled one over on everyone else in the family.

Provide a Writing Space

Every child needs a place to write. It could be a corner of his bedroom or a child-sized table in a family room. Be sure it is well lighted and large enough; the larger the writing surface the better. From their earliest years give children gifts associated with writing. Their space should be filled with pens and pencils of various kinds, pads of paper, stationery, and envelopes. Include a bound booklet for a diary or daily journal and a dictionary appropriate to the child's age. For older children a thesaurus is helpful. A Bible atlas, a Bible handbook, and a Bible dictionary will be basic tools if you use the family commentary ideas from Chapter 2.

A home computer will naturally be of interest to children because of the possibility of game playing, but it can also be a great tool to encourage writing. Show them how to boot up your word-processing program and encourage them to use the computer for school reports, letters, and other types of writing.

Various programs for encouraging children to write are also available. Some programs include a variety of graphics backgrounds on which the user can superimpose clip-art images. The story to accompany the illustrations can be added at the bottom of each page, and when all the text and graphics are in place children can even add a musical score.

Provide a Writing Time

"Just as you would not expect your child to become a pianist without daily piano practice or a good reader without daily reading sessions, you cannot expect your child to be an accomplished writer without a great deal of practice," says Linda Lamme.

Children are great imitators. They will want to write if they see Mom and Dad writing. Since there are certain writing tasks that must be done on a regular basis, set aside a particular time each day for those tasks and make it a family time. Parents can catch up on correspondence or write checks to pay bills (a necessary form of writing). Children can do any project they wish, but for that time period everyone writes.

Provide the Tools for Writing

Even before children begin formal education they will enjoy using the tools of writing. Stretch out the largest piece of brown wrapping paper or blank newsprint you can find; provide a variety of colored pens, pencils, or crayons; and turn the children loose. If you have been reading to them regularly, they will start to imitate the shapes of letters. You could also write their name for them in large letters and let them practice making copies of it all over the paper.

Many children will start to write as soon as they become aware of the fact that letters illustrate sounds. An elementary writing teacher tells about a boy who began writing at age five. One day he wrote a note to his mother, who, busy talking with friends, had not noticed that he was trying to ask her something. Failing to get her attention, he wrote on a piece of paper: RUDF. Even though the note didn't seem to make sense, his mother was perceptive enough to decode it—*Are you deaf?*—and then to understand its importance and to respond to the needs of her child.

Make Writing Important

Children will place the same value on writing that their parents do. The National Council of Teachers of English suggests, "Praise the child's efforts at writing. Forget what happened to you in school and resist the tendency to focus on errors of spelling, punctuation, and other mechanical aspects of writing. Emphasize the child's successes."

One way to show the value you place on your child's writing is to ask for writing as a gift. Since children seldom have great amounts of money to spend on gifts, they will like the idea of giving a gift that doesn't cost anything. You, in turn, will be happy to receive a poem or story to treasure instead of another tie you don't need.

Write a Pleasure Book

At the end of each day have each person write down something pleasant that happened that day. It might be that the first flowers of the season bloomed. Maybe a letter was received from a favorite cousin. Possibly a Scripture verse or a remark from the pastor's message at church was a special blessing. The entire exercise takes very little time, but it puts each member of the family on the alert, watching for those good things that happen to all of us every day. Keep the book near the dining room table and pass it around just as the meal is ending, or take it from room to room as you stop in to say good night and have prayer with the children before turning off the light.

Write to Predict Endings

Many of the cartoons in your newspaper have continued story lines. Read them with your children and then have each person predict what he thinks will happen in the strip the following day. You could even draw your own versions and then compare them with the author's the next day to see whose idea is nearest to the author's. Lee and Rudman suggest this activity in *Mind over Media* (New York: Seaview Books, 1982). They conclude, "The ability to predict endings is another reading skill that is all too often practiced in a dull way with school texts. Skills practiced in amusing or entertaining ways are better remembered."

Write Secret Messages

Writing in code is a fascinating pastime for children of all ages. Leave messages in code when you need to be away from home, and you can be certain they will be read. There are many simple codes that can be used.

1. Use the next letter in the alphabet to stand for its neighbor.

   Q V U P V U U I F U S B T I

   means PUT OUT THE TRASH.

2. An interesting variation is to turn the letters of the alphabet around so that Z equals A, Y equals B, X equals C, and so on.

   DV OLEV BLF EVIB NFXS

   means WE LOVE YOU VERY MUCH.

3. For a backwards code you simply write every word in reverse, arranging the word order in reverse as well.

   EIKOOC A EVAH NAC UOY DNA ONAIP RUOY ECITCARP

   means PRACTICE YOUR PIANO AND YOU CAN HAVE A COOKIE.

4. Leave all of the words in order but put the spaces in the wrong places.

   MAR CYC ALLE DFO RYO UAN DWAN TSYO UTOC ALLHE RBA CK

   means MARCY CALLED FOR YOU AND WANTS YOU TO CALL HER BACK.

5. Numbers can be substituted for letters. 1 equals A, 2 equals B, 3 equals C, and so on through the alphabet.

   23,5,1,18,5,7,18,15,3,5,18,25,19,8,15,16,16,9,14,7.

   Work that one out for yourself.

6. By drawing up a simple decoder, you can make symbols of various kinds stand for letters of the alphabet. We left the first message for the children one Saturday morning

25

when they were all still in bed and received the second one (using our code) later that same day.

7. Closely related to writing in code is writing with invisible ink. Here the message does not need to be scrambled, but the recipient must know how to reveal the invisible message.

One of the simplest forms of invisible ink is lemon juice. Use a calligraphy pen or a toothpick with lemon juice to write on paper, and the message will appear only when the paper is pressed with a very hot iron. Thank-you notes, invitations, and secret messages to friends can all be prepared in this fashion, but don't forget to include instructions or they will think you have enclosed the wrong piece of paper.

Make Lists

Have children help make grocery lists, lists of things they would like to receive for Christmas or a birthday, or lists of places they would like to go on vacation. The Marc Moffitt family has a weekly "Family Night" in which each child makes the choice of what they will do together on that evening. So his son Andrew made a list of ideas for the days he got to choose.

1. Go camping.
2. Go swimming.
3. Have a picnic.
4. Sleep outside.
5. Get my shoes.
6. Slumber party.
7. Hot rice and raisins.

Make up your own list of ideas or try any of the following:

- all the states seen on license plates while traveling
- all the verses referred to during a sermon at church
- all the words in road signs that begin with "M"
- the names of all cousins
- the names of God discovered in Bible reading
- the names of all instruments recognized during a band or orchestra concert
- all the gospel choruses known by heart

Write Memo Boards

A central communications board is often a necessity for a family as the teen years arrive and family members are increasingly involved in school, church, and social functions. But even when children are small, a memo board can be a source of interactive writing activities. A chalkboard mounted in a central location, a bulletin board with paper and thumb tacks readily available, or even the door of the refrigerator can be used. If the refrigerator is the central location in your home, provide magnets, sticky notes, or a marking pen with ink that can be wiped off.

In a delightful article in the October 1989 *Reader's Digest*, John Hubbell extols the praises of the sticky note. "In my pantheon of heroes," he says, "the man who invented stickum notepads ranks right up there next to Alexander Graham Bell." Hubbell, with tongue firmly in cheek, asserts, "Thanks to the stickums, my family has learned to produce concise, meaningful messages."

The rest of the article illustrates how his family has learned this lesson. One example will suffice. An unsigned message appeared on the wall above the telephone: *Jim called.* "We know a lot of Jims," says Hubbell. "No one had any idea which Jim had called, and no one would accept credit for taking the message. It stayed on the cupboard for weeks."

A memo board may not solve all of your telephone message disasters, but it can provide for different forms of family communication. A memo board will be most effective if used for two-way communication. Write questions and answers, jokes and poems to be completed, and "feel-good" messages that will generate similar responses.

Linda Lamme in *Growing Up Writing* (Washington, D.C.: Acropolis Books, 1984) tells how parents in one family wrote secret messages to their daughter each day. They were secret because the child could not yet read. These parents would read the messages to their daughter and she would quickly memorize them. Whenever visitors came to the house or baby sitters arrived, the child would bring them to her room to read her secret messages to them. What a wonderful way to teach a child the importance of writing.

Keep a Diary

Keeping a diary or journal is a type of informal writing that will never be graded, can be completely personal, and yet provides invaluable daily writing practice. Often a child will begin a diary because of the example of someone else or because it is given as a gift. It is really not important what is recorded in a diary; the very act of recording events, people, and emotions is valuable in itself.

I was given a five-year diary for Christmas and kept diaries regularly for the next eleven years. Many of the entries were rather mundane, items like "I went to the library," and "The swimming pool was cleaned." On other days the important events were world news, like on November 22, 1963.

> *Kennedy was assassinated!!! About noon in Dallas. A communist sympathizer. Heard about it at school. Virginia Chambers wedding.*

Like others who were alive in 1963, I remember exactly where I was when I heard the news that President Kennedy had been shot. But I certainly didn't remember attending a wedding that evening.

Some days stand out only in retrospect, like the weekend I met my bride to be, Carmen Odens.

> *November 6, 1965. Twelve boys left here at 8.00 and arrived in Redwood Falls at 10:30. Did some canvassing for Pastor Odens both this morning and this afternoon. Tonight there was a fellowship banquet at the church. I led singing and played "Send the Light."*
>
> *November 7, 1965. Played my trumpet three times led singing twice and played the piano for Dwight Turbot. Went to the park this afternoon and fell in the river (just wet feet). Carmen Odens showed us around. Junior in high school and very nice.*

Family vacations or trips of any kind are excellent times to keep travel journals. Even though you may take many pictures, the sounds and smells and sights of unusual places will escape you if you fail to record them at the time they are experienced.

Lorene Gibbons kept a journal of a trip to Bible lands and Europe to see the Oberammergau Passion Play during the summer of 1990. Her memories capture the essence of a young girl's first time abroad. Each evening she chose a particular event and made it the title for that day. May 30th was "Missing Gorbachev and Other Small Heartaches" because the tour group left Minnesota on the same day the Russian leader arrived for a visit. June 2nd, when the Intifada called a half-day strike in Jerusalem, her entry was titled, "Vendor Wars in the Late 20th Century." June 3rd was "In Guide We Trust."

Here is a selection from June 1st called "The 220 Volt Blues."

Amman, Jordan
6:30 A.M.

The entire city is built among the tops of the hills, and everything is constructed out of the same white limestone, a local rock. The city sparkles in the sun as I lean against the iron balcony rail. It is a city like no other I have ever seen — utterly foreign and exotically beautiful.

My thoughts are interrupted by an anguished cry echoing from inside our room. I fought my way back through the sheers and found Heather staring disconsolately at her hair dryer. "What's wrong?" I asked.

"I think I blew out my hair dryer."

Vague recollections floated through my mind. "Um, I think the voltage is higher than in the U.S., or something."

"Well, I'm going to try plugging in my curling iron, OK?"

"I don't know," I said doubtfully.

"Well, I'll try it."

It melted!

Make Greeting Cards

Making greeting cards is an excellent family activity. Chapter 7 will be devoted entirely to creating unique family Christmas cards, but holidays come almost every month; so don't confine this activity to Christmas. The text for cards may be serious or humorous, short or long, prose or poetry. Illustrations may be original or cut from other sources.

Computer-generated graphics can make the preparation of special occasion greetings more professional looking, and older children may tend to use more words than beginning writers. The following Valentine's Day greeting was prepared by Chad on his computer when he was 19.

Dear Family,

With Valentine's Day upon us, I felt a strong desire to share with you my appreciation for all that you have done for me and meant to me. Your love for me and your confidence in my abilities has done more than I can ever repay you for. Thank you for all the times you have shared with me, the fun times and the serious times, the times spent learning, and the times spent accomplishing what seemed like nothing, when we actually were able to grow closer to each other.

Because of these feelings, (combined with a recognition of the rising cost of store-bought cards), I decided to follow my wonderful Grandparents example and create, (with the help of my indispensable dorm companion, lovingly referred to as idc), a personal valentine for all of you. Besides, they always say that the home-made ones mean more anyway.

Finally, as proof of my appreciation for the previously mentioned character traits, I formally present to my favorite family, this small award.

HAPPY VALENTINES DAY

Chad

Write Name Cards

The relatives are gathering for Thanksgiving dinner, and the table is all set, complete with a name tag at every place. Children enjoy names and love to organize people; so creating name tags is fun. In one family the children didn't wait for special occasions; at almost every meal, name place cards were used to produce different seating arrangements for the family.

Name tags are also useful at a party that includes people who don't know each other. For a birthday party they can be decorated with a simple toy that will give each guest something to take home. Tags for gift packages can be individualized with special messages such as "To the best (and only) sister I've ever had."

Make Signs

At one time or another every child posts a sign on the bedroom door: "Keep Out." But signs can be used in a variety of ways. When children are at the stage where they are establishing daily habits such as making their bed and brushing their teeth, signs can be helpful and gentle reminders concerning those tasks. One teen-ager hung a large sign on the wall next to his bed that read, "No Bible, No Breakfast." It reminded him of the importance of a daily devotional time before other activities began.

Signs are important in play because they have the ability to transform ordinary objects into the extraordinary. Hang a sign on a tree house and it becomes a castle, rocket ship, hospital, or pirate ship. Hang a sign on the front door and the entire house becomes a vacation hideaway on the Florida seacoast or a Colorado ski-country chalet.

Write Family Stories

Every family needs to become the preserver of its own history. There are stories about members of your family that are unique, but they will be forgotten if no one takes the time to write them down.

From the cute sayings the children used when they first learned to talk, to the last words of the aged, family memories need to be preserved.

When our children were small, they began to use the contraction "amn't," as in "I amn't sure I want to wear shoes today." Although at the time we tried to correct them, that word has now become a part of family history that we would not want to forget.

Claire Fitch shared the following story concerning her Uncle Herb. It is a good example of a story that is significant only to those who know her uncle, but for them it recounts a part of their family history that should not be lost. She told how Herb stopped along the road to pick up a dead raccoon whose pelt seemed to be in good shape. When he placed it in the trunk of his car, it woke up. A fierce battle followed, but Herb won.

One word of advice that is always given to beginning writers is, "Write about subjects you already know." Since your family knows each other, it is natural for them to write about each other. One of Chad's first stories was about his brother.

Kent, the Willing Worker

Kent was a little boy. He always wanted to work. Wherever he could help someone he would help them. He helped mommy sweep the floor. He helped Tommy get up when she fell down. He even helped daddy get Wendys doll house down from its shelf and put it up again. It is very heavy. And would you believe? He is only four years old. The end.
by Chad

Many parents invent stories to satisfy a child's insatiable thirst for storytelling, particularly at bedtime. My brother and I were raised on an entire series of "Jick and Jock" stories told by our mother, but because they were never written down, not much more than the boys' names has been preserved in our memories. Having invented some "Jick and Jock" stories for my own children, I recorded them on cassette tape and gave out copies. That way the stories would be preserved and the kids could listen to them anytime they wanted. More than once they have fallen asleep with the tape player running.

Jick and Jock were ideal for a serial story because they lived in Montana, where my brother and I had been raised, and their adventures closely paralleled our experiences in childhood. They had one advantage over us, however; they were not limited by reality. Where my brother David had only pretended to hunt alligators in the backwater of the Yellowstone River, Jick and Jock actually captured them. We played at knights and castles and dragons in the foothills above town, but Jick and Jock met dragons—even one who knew how to play the game of Uno.

Not only did the "Jick and Jock" stories mirror the childhood experiences I had enjoyed, but they also proved useful in solving problems our children were facing. The story of the dragon who played Uno emerged at a time when playing that game was the favorite pastime of the entire family. The problem was that some of the children had a very difficult time losing. They were not good sports. In the story, Jick and Jock agreed to play Uno with their new friend, the dragon, but they soon discovered that if he ever lost he blew fire out of his mouth and burned up all the cards. He was the ultimate poor sport, the one who ruins the game for everyone else. It was a subtle lesson but one that made its point.

Write for Information

Letters written for the purpose of obtaining information will often result in a flood of mail that children enjoy receiving. Our children have written to other states to obtain information on potential travel destinations. Before we made a move from Virginia to Montana, they wrote to the Chamber of Commerce in Missoula and received a large packet of materials concerning the state and city they were about to call home. They have also written to mission boards requesting information for reports on foreign countries. Letters to congressmen have brought personal replies as well as answers to questions.

Write to Favorite People

You can also encourage children to write to favorite authors. If they are reading the "Mandie" series, have them write to Lois Gladys Leppard in care of the publisher. If their current interest is the "Sugar Creek Gang," they can write to Paul Hutchens. Authors usually respond to fan mail, and your children will enjoy hearing from those whose stories are their favorites.

Be sure to have your letter writer enclose a self-addressed stamped envelope and help him keep the name and address legible. Lack of a legible return address has been the cause of more than one disappointment. Encourage your child to share a personal response to the book instead of simply asking generic questions such as "Where do you get your ideas?"

Personal correspondence from children will be much appreciated by older relatives. Encourage your children to share specific incidents, accounts of baseball and basketball games, events from summer camp, and stories of family happenings. Don't require such letters, but make sure they see the letters the family receives from relatives and leave your own letters open in a central location before sending them so that children can add a note, original drawing, or letter of their own.

Write Original Stories

Children begin telling stories before they can write, so their earliest stories will need to be transcribed. Either write them down as they are told or record them on cassette or videotape and write out the story later. It will seem much more like a story to them if you actually take the time to write out the story and the child can see it on paper.

Usually children need only a nudge to get them started writing. Here are just some of the ways that you can give that nudge.

- Write a story from a title provided by an adult:
    My First Doll
    My First Day of School
- Write a story about a picture.
- Write a story you have heard, but change the ending.
- Write a story about a trip or experience.

An Embarassing Accident

Once in Virginia my family was having a picnic in our backyard. I went into the house for awhile to get a drink. When I went in, I laid my plate on the chair I was sitting on. When I came back to the picnic I accidentally forgot about my food and I sat down right in my plate! I got really embarassed and I had to go back inside, change my clothes, and get more food. Everyone in my family laughed at me, but I couldn't help it, I was only four. This experience has taught me a lesson I'll never forget.

by Tammy, age 10

- Write to finish a sentence.
    If I were a _____.
    Once upon a time in Alaska I saw a _____.
- Write a cartoon strip.

- Write to supply the ending for a story.
- Write a biography of parents, siblings, a pet, a wild animal, or a fictional or historical character.

Here is a young girl's biography of Ruth, complete with the original spellings, capitalization, and punctuation.

The Story of Ruth

Once more there was a famine in the land and a farmer decided to move his family from Bethlehem where they lived to Moab where it was easier to grow corn. The farmer and his two sons died after a time, and the farmer's wife, naomi, made up her mind that she would go back home. the two sons had married in Moab their wives were called Orpah and Ruth. when naomi told orpah and Ruth she was going home they said they would go part of the way with her. presently Naomi said it was time for them to go back. orpah kissed her and was ready to return to moab, but Ruth said, "do not ask me to leave you, or to go back again. Where you go, I will go; and where you live, I will live. your people shall be my people, and your God shall be my God."

Wendy, age 8

- Write a story pretending to be a favorite character.
- Write a mystery story.
- Write a newspaper account of a Bible story.
- Write a letter to a friend as if you were a Bible character.
- Write a story pretending to be an animal.
- Write about traveling someplace you've never visited.
- Write a legend.

- Write about visiting another period of history through time travel.
- Write to heal. Physicians often recommend writing as part of the healing process. Patients are encouraged to draw pictures or write stories that illustrate their hurts and the way they are dealing with the world about them.

One teen-age girl had been under treatment for anorexia when she wrote this story for her father.

Flame of Love

There once was a little candle that burned with a bright and cheerful flame. The flame was small but very strong and true. There was a problem though — no one could see that flame because the candle was kept in a sunny room. Then one day the little candle was moved into a dark, drafty, cold room. The candle grew very cold and shivered. The flame flickered. The darkness was frightening and lonely to the candle. In fear and desperation the candle tried to hide. The flame flickered again. Then a strong draft blew across the room — oppressing the candle. The fragile flame almost went out. Now the candle was desperate and looked around for help. Across the room on a different shelf sat a glass lantern cover.

"Oh," cried the candle, "If only I had the glass around me, protecting me, I would not be so weak. The candle begged and pleaded with the lantern cover but it wouldn't listen. The flame was now just a feeble spark, barely visible. Pain filled the heart of the little candle.

Then slowly, quietly the glass cover rose from its place on the shelf and came over to the candle. Quietly the cover rested over and around the dying spark. The candle and spark were now protected, nurtured and supported. Once again the spark grew into a flame. The candle was still in the dark, but the flame grew so strong and bright it shone out into the darkness. The once black spaces were now just dim and the dim spaces light. Just because the weak, struggling spark, when protected, grew into a strong, shining flame.

I am the candle. My love of life (my spirit) is the flame. Anorexia, bulimia, abuse, and depression are the elements in the closet. Dad is the glass cover.

The girl's father says that years later he still cries when he reads what she wrote. Just writing down her feelings became the means of encouragement for both her and her father.

Encourage someone to write today, whether a child or a parent or yourself. Of all the messages a family shares, only those that are recorded will be preserved for future generations to enjoy. Start writing "write away!"

Write On

Learning to write is basically learning to have fun with language. It is fascinating to think that God chose written language as His primary means of communication to mankind. In this age of communication with the computer revolution, the fax machine, the video industry, and radio and television, writing remains at the top of business-skills lists. At the same time, words can be fun.

A family that has fun with words is well on the way to a place of serving others through writing. This chapter provides a variety of games that can be played with words. Our family has used many of them while traveling. Others creep into everyday conversation around the dinner table. After playing word games, your family may discover humor in unexpected places. While we were sitting in church one Sunday, the minister invited us to "turn in your Bibles." I grinned to myself about the possible connotations of such a remark and then glanced down to see Kent and Tammy passing their Bibles, "turning them in" to Mother. Later someone shared the incident with the minister, and he has been trying ever since to find ways to avoid that particular cliché.

Play "I Spy"

One of the earliest word games that can be played with children is "I Spy." Although it is not technically a writing game, since nothing is written down, it still increases an awareness of language and observation. The person who is "it" chooses an object he can see and then says, "I spy something green" (or blue or white or gray, depending on the color). Then everyone else tries to guess what that person spied. The one who guesses right is "it" for the next round.

"I Spy" makes an excellent travel game with some simple rules. It is good to specify whether the object is inside or outside the car. If it is outside, the object should be far enough down the road so it can be guessed before you have left it miles behind. Also, be certain that everyone realizes he must choose a specific object before he names the color. There has always been a strong suspicion on the part of Chad, Wendy, and Kent that their youngest sister Tammy didn't make her choices until after they had named everything "green" that they could spy.

Make Travel Lists

The most familiar version of this game involves listing the states spotted on license plates as you travel. After playing the game for many years, the family came close to winning it during a summer vacation to Yellowstone Park. By the time the week was over only one state remained, Tennessee. Imagine our surprise the last night of vacation when we pulled into a campsite in Gallatin Gateway, Montana, and parked next to a van from Tennessee. But then imagine the greater surprise of that family when they looked out of their windows and saw five people crowded around the back of their vehicle for a photograph.

Travel lists don't have to be confined to license plates. Lists may be compiled of different kinds of animals or different numbers of animals. Grandpa Allen always told the children that the fastest way to obtain the total number of cows in a field was to count their legs and divide by four. By assigning different sides of the highway to teams of children, you can make the listing into a contest. Names of eating establishments could be listed, like "Dew Drop Inn," the "Owl Cafe," or the "Bloody Bucket." One family in the West spent years putting together a list of all the cattle brands they had seen.

Choose a Word for the Day

This can be a hilarious game for a long trip, although it may be used around the house as well. It begins when someone designates a common word such as "water" that will not be allowed in any form during conversation. Punishment or reward for using the word could take several forms. When a person says the word, everyone else can scream and holler. An alternative is to keep track of how many times each person slips and uses the word and then reward the one best able to control his tongue.

Play the Alphabet Game

Your family has probably been playing this game since the children first began to identify letters. As you travel, each person must find a word that begins with successive letters of the alphabet, and woe be to the person who comes to Q or X when you are not in the city. After playing the game an infinite number of times, the players will begin inventing alternatives in self-defense. Go through the alphabet backwards. Assign each child a side of the road and allow only those signs on his side to be used. Spell out a long word like "antidisestablishmentarianism." Alternate letters in the alphabet: the first person finds A, the second B, and so forth.

Write Riddles

Riddles often find their reason for existence in the double meanings that can be given to many words. Since the form of the riddle is usually question-and-answer, children quickly learn to invent their own. Their first attempts may not fit an adult concept of what a riddle should be, but endure the early stages of learning the form, and genuine humor will result. Tammy had a favorite riddle at age five. Her question whenever the other children started telling riddles was always the same, "How did the squirrel climb up the tree?" The answer to the riddle depended on her current whim, but to her they were all funny. She would giggle just as hard when she answered it "with his long tail" as she did when she said "with his acorns."

Actually, rewriting old riddles is an excellent way to learn about language. Harvey Wiener in *Any Child Can Write* (New York: Bantam Books, 1990) tells of a young writer who revised the riddle

Why do cows eat grass standing up?
Grass cannot sit down.

Using the same question, he changed the answer, thus creating an entirely new riddle.

Why do cows eat grass standing up?
There would be no room at the dinner table for the rest of us.

To get your family started writing riddles, read these "oldies but goodies" and change the answers to create your own versions.

What has four wheels and flies?
A garbage truck.

Why did the boy throw his clock out the window?
To see time fly.

What has an eye but cannot see?
A needle.

What has a hundred legs, but can't walk a single step?
Fifty pairs of pants.

It is also possible to create a new riddle by changing the question or by changing both the question and the answer.

Why did the dog cross the road?
To get to the other side.

Why did Hannibal cross the Alps?
To get to the other side.

Write Reversies

Usually, spelling a word backward produces nonsense: "boy" becomes "yob." But reversing some words produces a different word, for example, "drab" becomes "bard." To make this into a game, write a clue for the first form of the word and suggest the word that it will become in reverse. For "drab" and "bard" the clue could read like this: "What is a dull, yellowish-brown color forward and an ancient poet in reverse?"

Thinking of the words "tar" and "rat" you could write this clue: "What is used to build roads forward and scares mother to death in reverse?"

Once you begin playing this game, you set yourself up for some real surprises. One of the children stumped all of us with this clue: "What is a brand of foreign car forward and a complete sentence describing something that goes to school in reverse?"

After cudgeling our brains for a full thirty seconds we admitted defeat and were rewarded with this delightful reversie. "Forward the word is SUBARU and in reverse it is U R A BUS."

Here is a list of reversible word pairs to get your family started. Write clues for these and begin searching for your own.

nap—pan	not—ton
yard—dray	no—on
drawer—reward	tool—loot
stop—pots	liar—rail
live—evil	net—ten
saw—was	lap—pal
now—won	sub—bus

There's even an occasional word that can be turned upside down and still make sense like "MOM" and "WOW." That would have to be called a double reversie.

Write Palindromes

A word game similar to the reversie is the palindrome, a word or sentence that reads exactly the same either forward or backward, like "Bob" and "Otto" and "Hannah." One of the classic palindromes is the sentence supposedly spoken by Napoleon when he was sent into exile: "Able was I ere I saw Elba." Another is the mythical first sentence that Adam ever spoke to Eve: "Madam, in Eden I'm Adam."

Here are some words to get you started. Put them together in longer combinations with reversible words from the previous game and create your own palindromes.

mom	pop
civic	huh
dad	sis
did	kayak
Anna	a Toyota

With some practice you can begin creating entire palindromic sentences like these from an article by Sid McMeans.

"Won't pews fill if swept now?"

"No, it is opposition."

"So, Ida, adios."

"El Sid, do not race cart on odd isle."

Write an Advice Column

This is a good use for your family bulletin board or a possible column for a family newspaper. Appoint a different columnist each week or two and have him answer problems submitted anonymously by other members of the family. The columnist could also use a fake name of his own choosing and advertise for business at the beginning of his tenure as columnist.

COME ONE, COME ALL—

SEND YOUR QUESTIONS TO THE KNOW-IT-ALL!

"Dear Know-It-All, I have a problem getting out of bed in the morning. What should I do? (Signed) Lazy Bones."

"Dear Lazy Bones, Have you tried staying up all night?"

Write "Tom Swifties"

When author Edward Stratemeyer created his fictional hero, Tom Swift, he had no idea he was creating a word game as well. Tom was never content to simply "say" something during his adventures, he always said it "daringly" or "energetically" or "proudly." Most of the quotations referred to as "Tom Swifties" didn't appear in Stratemeyer's books. They are deliberate puns matching a quotation with a suitably punny adverb. Enjoy the following and then set out to create your own.

"I'll give you a hand," Tom said disarmingly.

"Let's go camping," Tom said intently.

"Care for a bon-bon?" Tom said sweetly.

"Bring me the scissors," Tom said pointedly.

"I like Beethoven's music the best," Tom said composedly.

Play the Dictionary Game

This game will provide a family or other group countless hours of entertainment, and you might even learn some useful information in the process. Dig out the largest dictionary you can find in the house and have someone look up a word that no one recognizes: something like "purfling." After the word has been chosen, everyone should write it down on his own piece of paper and next to it, a fictitious definition. The person who chose the word should write the correct definition on his paper and then collect the rest of the papers. After that person reads all the definitions to the group, everyone must vote for the definition he thinks is right. Since a person gets points for each vote his definition receives, voting for your own definition is not allowed. What would you choose as the correct definition for "purfling"?

Purfling: a term of measurement based on how far you can throw a cat.

Purfling: an old Italian word for purse-snatching.

Purfling: the inlaid border of a violin.

Purfling: an intricate maneuver in the sport of surfing.

Purfling: the scientific name for the daffodil in a condition agitated by excessive amounts of water.

Purfling: the runt in a family of birds.

Purfling: a sport in which you see how far you can fling a nerf shotput without bending your elbow.

Purfling: tearing perforations off computer paper.

The answers are frequently and sometimes deliberately humorous, as you can see. The correct definition of purfling? It is the inlaid border of a violin.

After everyone has voted, the score should be tallied. Each vote for a fictional definition counts one for the person who wrote it. A vote for the right definition gives a person one point. If no one votes for the correct definition, then the person who chose the word gets five points. The game can go on forever, but a convenient stopping point comes when each participant has had one opportunity to choose a word.

To play a variation of the dictionary game at a youth activity or Sunday school party, use a Bible dictionary as the source of your words.

Write a Scavenger Hunt

In the typical scavenger hunt, a team searches for a certain list of objects that must be discovered within a time limit. After children have participated in the game several times, give them the job of making up their own list for the next party you host. As they grow older, there are variations on the typical game that will make it a continual favorite.

One variation is to provide each team with a tape recorder and give them a list of sounds that they must collect on tape.

a police siren

the sound of a cow mooing

the click of a traffic light as it changes color

the city mayor introducing himself

the chirping of a bird

a radio announcer giving the temperature

With younger children, the game can be played by recording the sounds in advance and then having them listen and try to identify as many of the sounds as possible. In this version of the game it is best to use familiar sounds.

the ringing of the telephone

the whir of the clothes dryer

the sound of an electric typewriter

the voice of a family member or favorite visitor

the splash of running water

A great favorite with youth groups is the mall scavenger hunt. Not more than a day before the activity (to minimize the possibility of prices and signs changing) the writer of the game must go through the mall and identify all of the items to be "found." The same clues are distributed to each team, but the order should be changed to avoid large congregations of people in stores that are trying to conduct business. If drivers are available, the game could be played with an entire city as the playground. Here are some examples:

You're thirsty. While waiting for the people at Orange Julius to make you a Super Deluxe you decide to count the oranges in the display case. But you get only the ones on the left of the hot dogs counted before your drink is ready. How many did you count?

You want to find out who won the basketball game this morning. Since you have just been eating banana-cream pie at Pioneer Pies, you consult their available newspapers. What newspapers are you able to purchase from the stands in front of the restaurant?

Grizzlies Don't Come Easy, by Ralph Young. Sound interesting? I knew you were just dying to read it. So how do you find it? Look up the call number, of course. When you have the number, forget the book. All you need is the number.

Another version of the scavenger hunt is to give each team an instant camera and have members take pictures of various objects around town. Whatever version you use, have fun writing out the directions.

Write a Mystery Game

Many versions of mystery games are available through toy stores, but writing your own will allow you to adapt it to your own situation. The first time we tried this game, about thirty people participated at a cast party held after the final performance of a college production. For over two hours the questions continued non-stop until each one identified a suspect in the "murder."

Using an event from Bible history as the starting point for your mystery will enable the participants to increase their knowledge of Scripture at the same time they are enjoying the game. Take the death of King Amon, for example, recorded in II Chronicles 33:24: "And his servants conspired against him and slew him in his own house."

The first step in preparing your mystery is to write a narration that gives the background and setting for the occasion. This narration will be provided to every participant in the game.

Amon succeeded his father as king when he was twenty-two years old. During the first year of his reign, people were excited about the change since his father Manasseh had been king for fifty-two years. But the novelty soon wore off, and by the end of his second year there were many who felt that his coronation had been a mistake. He refused to worship in the temple and had altars to the sun and moon built in the outer courtyard of the palace. He allowed the Baal worshippers to practice their religion in public. There were even rumors that he had consulted with a witch and that he was planning to sacrifice his son Josiah by fire in the valley of Hinnom.

On the second anniversary of his coronation, King Amon hosted a celebration in the palace. The feasting continued until long past midnight. The next morning a palace guard discovered the body of the king in a remote corner of the garden. He had been stabbed in the back.

This particular account was based in part on the story of Amon in II Kings 21. Be sure you don't change the facts as they are presented in Scripture, but feel free to give details not mentioned in the Bible that easily could have happened but are not recorded. During the writing of the opening narration be careful not to give away the identity of the murderer; instead show how it would have been possible for anyone to perpetrate the crime. The identity of the murderer is what must be discovered by the participants in the game.

Your next project as a writer of this mystery game will be to create a biographical sketch for each person who attended the palace celebration. The suspects will be impersonated by the participants. The game will be more fun if each person is included, so try to write a biography for everyone. Since we already know that the murderers were among the servants, some of the people you write about in the biographies will not be suspects. If you are writing for younger children, or if this is the first time a group has played a similar game, it will probably be better to limit the suspects to no more than six anyway.

Each biography should contain a list of personal characteristics, a description of where that person was at the time of the murder, a plausible but flawed alibi if guilty, and clues to the murder that they alone possess.

For the murder of King Amon, biographies should be written for Prince Josiah, Queen Jedidah, the Queen Mother Meshullemeth, High Priest Hilkiah, and a great variety of guests, guards, servers, cooks, attendants, priests, soldiers, and entertainers. Since a biographical sketch is read only by the person who receives it, the only ones who will know that they are the murderers are those impersonating servants who are labeled guilty and provided with an alibi.

These biographies are the first ones that should be written. Describe the murderers in detail. Tell them what clothes they wore, how they planned and executed the crime, where they were during the rest of the celebration, and what they did to cover up their criminal activity. Once you have completed the biographies of the murderers, write all the rest, giving each person at least one clue to who actually committed the crime. A sample biography for one of the servants would read as follows.

> Name: Maaz. You are a servant to King Amon with the primary responsibility of tasting everything he eats before it is served to him. You are 37, and you served in the same capacity for King Manasseh, as did your father before you. At the celebration last evening, you personally served the king. When the feasting was over, you retired to your room in the servant's wing of the palace and stayed there the rest of the night. You are not married, so you have no wife to vouch for your innocence, but you spoke briefly with the guard at the gate when you left, and you are certain he will remember that you were gone before the crime was committed. You also know that in addition to the guards, who all carry daggers, there was one other person who had a weapon at the celebration. That was the cook, named Hanan.

As you are writing each biography, include a detail that would implicate them in the crime and an alibi that would extricate them from accusation. The cook, Hanan, for example could explain that he carried the dagger in order to carve the beef that was hanging over the pit in the garden. If you decided that the cook was one of the murderers, his alibi could include the other conspirator, who would swear that he was in the kitchen at the time of the crime.

While writing the biographies, think about the people who will be participating in the game. Write biographies that will fit both men and women. If you know that someone is outgoing, you might want to assign them the part of a traveling musician or juggler who is hired to entertain at the celebration. Some people will be able to take any part and enjoy acting a character while others will prefer a personality similar to their own.

After all the biographies have been written, type them on separate sheets of paper and your preparation is finished. As you distribute them for the game, inform the participants that they are free to embellish the biography they have been given, but they should do it without lying. For example, they don't need to give a detailed description of the entire evening to someone who asks them where they were the previous evening. Instead they may share only a portion of their activities. This will be particularly necessary in the case of the culprits because they will do their best to remain undiscovered.

After players are familiar with the biographies they have received, the game can develop in one of two ways. You may simply turn all the players loose and tell them to discover the murderers by asking questions. That approach will work well with a crowd of older teens or adults.

Another way is to have each person announce his or her assigned name and give a brief explanation of who he is and what he knows about the events surrounding the crime. After all the stories have been shared, open the meeting for questions that must be asked one at a time. This could last twenty to thirty minutes. Then have each person write down the name of the person he suspects. Finally, reveal the culprits and find out which detectives were able to piece together the clues correctly and solve the mystery.

Write Questionnaires

It is almost impossible to open a popular magazine without facing one or more questionnaires. These are designed to reveal everything from our attitudes toward politics to our aptitude for successful spelunking. Peter Stillman says, "I have unearthed evidence that they were invented by the medical profession to offset the effects of waiting, which was also invented by the medical profession."

To write a questionnaire, simply compose a series of short questions and follow those with a set of instructions for interpreting the results. To have fun with a questionnaire, be sure the questions are open to interpretation and the interpretation is open to questioning. The following questionnaire was prepared as the opening for an adult Sunday school class but could be adapted for a family gathering.

This questionnaire is based upon years of study concerning leadership. Place a check in the column under "yes" or "no" depending on how each answer best fits your attitudes, feelings, convictions, or inclinations at the present time.

Yes   No

_____ _____ 1. Have you ever caught a fish on a set line?

_____ _____ 2. Do you read a book while you watch TV?

_____ _____ 3. Should Moses have broken the Ten Commandments on Aaron's head?

_____ _____ 4. What kind of fish was it?

_____ _____ 5. Has spelunking ever played a major part in your life?

_____ _____ 6. Why do the stars shine only at night?

_____ _____ 7. Do you have a favorite earlobe?

_____ _____ 8. Can a person be a leader if no one follows?

_____ _____ 9. Does your favorite hymn begin with the words "Far away"?

_____ _____10. Do you have mixed feelings about your indecisiveness?

If you answered 'yes' to numbers 1, 3, 5, 7, 9 and 'no' to 2, 4, 6, 8, 10, you were guessing. If you answered "yes" to 1, 2, 7, 8 and 'no' to 3, 4, 5, 6, 9, then you skipped question 10. If you answered either 'yes' or 'no' to questions 4 and 6 you had better go back and read those questions again. If you refused to answer at all, it proves that you are not taking this questionnaire seriously.

What did the questionnaire have to do with leadership? Nothing. But it had everything to do with fun, and after having a bit of fun the group was ready to get serious.

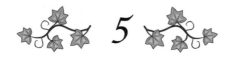

Writing the Family

Many families have started "round robin" letters, which are sent from one unit of an extended family to another until everyone has contributed. But the record may well be held by the Joe Josephs family of Alexandria, Minnesota. Begun in 1950 by this family of thirteen children, their round robin has traveled around the United States approximately four times a year for over forty years. As the letter comes to each family, they remove their previous contribution, add a new letter and send it quickly on its way. In that fashion each member of the family receives news from all the rest of the family at one time and can respond by writing one letter instead of twelve.

After the "robin" had been flying for twenty-five years, each member of the Josephs family received an unusual gift. Elmer, one of the brothers, had been making photocopies of each letter as it came to his house in Minneapolis. He bound these letters together according to families and returned them to their original writers. At the same time he encouraged each of his brothers and sisters to continue the practice of saving their own letters, reminding them that in this way they could accumulate a ready-made family history.

Our family of four has also tried to keep a "bird" flying for twenty years or so. To say the least, its flight has been erratic. It seems to nest in various parts of the country for long periods of hibernation. If it makes its flight even once a year, its coming is a matter for great celebration. But even with such a haphazard flight plan, the appearance of our "robin" brightens any day.

We all want to know what is happening in our families, and the telephone makes it much more easy than in past decades. But few families tap their telephone lines in order to preserve conversations for future reference. Some other method must be used in order to have a family record available for future generations.

A "round robin" is only one way that you can preserve family history. This chapter will provide many possible ways to accomplish the same task. The important thing to remember is that the sooner you start, the more you will accumulate.

Write Scrapbooks

One excellent method of preserving memories of your children's early years is scrapbooks.

One year during spring cleaning, my wife walked into Wendy's room and found the wastebasket overflowing with discarded school papers, award certificates, and birthday cards. Without saying a word she carried the contents of the entire basket up into the attic and added them to a box marked in large letters with Wendy's name. Next to that box sat another one for Chad, and next to that, one for Kent and one for Tammy.

To your children, the end of a school year is a time to clean house. To you it should be a time to store away highlights of the year for future reference. When your storage box begins to overflow it will be time to transfer those memories into a scrapbook, or maybe even two or three.

The following list of items collected for various scrapbooks could inspire your own collection.

- birth announcements
- cradle roll enrollment certificate
- a first valentine
- birthday cards
- a homemade valentine given to Mother
- a list of 36 gospel choruses Chad knew from memory when he was two years old
- Sunday school coloring projects, carefully dated by Mother
- original art work
- a four-year-old hand traced in pencil
- letters from relatives recalling such events as a bout with chicken pox
- report cards
- lists of Christmas gifts
- book reports
- piano recital programs
- early samples of writing, usually "Mom" and other names (Later samples, after school began, include such classics as "Daniel Boone," which Chad wrote in the first grade.)

Daniel Boone
Played a tune
On a horn
In the moon.
Daniel Boone
Came home soon
To eat a bear
Without the hair.
Daniel Boone
Killed a racoon
To make a hat
How about that?

by Chad

- play posters
- tee ball certificate
- a first song
- stories, such as Wendy's "The Mystery of the Moose on the Wall!"
- honor society inauguration certificate
- recipes (Wendy composed the following recipe for fudge when she was six. No one remembers for sure how it turned out, but maybe one of her children will discover it in the scrapbook and try it again some day.)

Fudge

1. milk $\frac{1}{2}$
2. brown sugar $\frac{2}{4}$
3. chocolate chips $\frac{2}{4}$
4. silver balls 4
5. stuff you make coconut out of
6. white sugar

- A list of events for a Good News club Wendy organized with all the kids in the neighborhood:

1. Rules
2. Songs
3. Bible verses
4. Play time
5. Bible story
6. Getting saved
7. Art
8. Games
9. Refreshments
10. Go home

- A note to Mother asking permission to spend time with a friend:

> Dear Mommy,
> Kari's mom said, If you are not home I am eating with Kari and Kari's mom said I could go shopping with them. If I can go shopping with her mark yes or no
> Yes_____   no_____
>
> Love, Wendy

As you can see, the list is endless. Begin today collecting your own scrapbook memories, and your scrapbook will increase in value every year. One scrapbook that belonged to my parents when they were dating in the early forties contained a faded telegram that read "Philippians 4:4." That was the entire message, but we all knew the story behind it.

When Mom and Dad were dating, Dad was asked to travel from Minnesota to Montana to hold a week of special meetings in the town of Baker. By the following Sunday the church had called him to be their pastor. Then came the sending of the telegram. Mom knew exactly what it meant. The story always ended the same way. "We came west on our honeymoon and have been on it ever since." To us as youngsters that telegram contained the assurance that our parents were and always would be in love.

Write Family Newsletters

Another way to make contact with an extended family is by means of family newsletters. Peter Stillman in *Families Writing* (Cincinnati: Writer's Digest Books, 1989) says, "Admit it; there isn't a single good reason why your family shouldn't tackle a project like *The Family News*." A family newsletter could circulate just to the members of your immediate family; it could be sent to all of the aunts, uncles, and cousins of your extended family; or it could become a welcome substitute for your annual Christmas letter and be sent to all your friends.

Elmer Josephs, the uncle who surprised his family with twenty-five years of their own letters, has been editing *S*T*A*A*R* Light* for over seven years. The Josephs family came to Minnesota from Finland with the family name of Stjerna, meaning "Star" in Finnish. However, there were so many Stjernas in northern Minnesota that several of the brothers decided to change their names. One branch of the family took the name Josephs and another Josephson.

S*T*A*A*R Light is mainly a genealogical newsletter. The big family project right now is raising money to pay for a translation of *The History of Kuusamo* from Finnish to English. "The *History* is a record of our ancestry, beginning in the year 1500," writes Elmer in the newsletter. "Perhaps no other family, unless of royal or noble birth, has been so thoroughly recorded as has been the Lappish/Finnish family of Stjerna."

A summary of the translation work already completed is included in each edition of *S*T*A*A*R Light,* and it provides a fascinating look at the family heritage.

Mother's sister, Bernice Nixon, contributed a Christmas memory to one edition of the newsletter.

> One of my favorite memories was the year Dad gave me ten cents for my Christmas shopping. After much thought I purchased a package of Juicy Fruit and a package of Black Jack gum. Wrapping each stick and deciding who should get that flavor took a lot of thought as well.

Games, poems, and current information about family members are also included in the newsletter, but the primary emphasis is on the Finnish roots of the "Stjerna Tribe and Associated Relatives."

A family-based newsletter we have enjoyed receiving comes from Kim Odens in West Springfield, Massachusetts. Kim produces a professional-looking newsletter on her home computer and calls it the *Springfield Gazette*. In addition to sending it to all of her cousins, she mails it to missionary children as well.

Kim's paper includes an account of a field trip to the "Eastern States Exhibition" with their home-school group. "Since there were six of us, we rode in two different police cars with the police chief and another policeman as our chauffeurs," she writes.

The arrival of the *Springfield Gazette* inspired Tammy to respond with her own computer-generated newsletter. She chose the name *Occasional Owatonnan* and soon had her first edition in the mail.

Springfield Gazette

Vol. 1, No. 1

September, 1990

Day by Day

Kim   busy with schoolwork and the computer; keeping up with piano practicing; babysitting

Kara   busy with schoolwork, typing, piano; outdoor activities

Kristi   playing dolls; busy with schoolwork; practicing the piano; collecting leaves

The Big E

On September 14 we went to the Big E. We rode half of the way in a police car with the chief of police.

One of the first things we did was look at the state buildings — one for each New England state. The buildings had a lot of good food. The Vermont building had a barbershop quartet and some sled dogs in it. It also had maple sugar in it. I bought some and it tasted good. Then we looked at all the shops in the street. We found one with coonskin hats for sale. There weren't a whole lot of good shops, so soon we went to the horse barn. As we were going in we saw a tiny horse hitched to a surrey go by. When we went into the barn we found that the horses could not be seen just then, so we went back and had lunch on a big lawn.

When we were done eating we got to the best part. We went to Funland to see all the rides and games. Games came first. It took me a while to pick out one, but I decided to try one where there was a big bunch of strings. Each one was connected to a little piece of wood with an S, M, or L on it (small, medium, or large prize). I pulled three strings and got three small prizes — a Mighty Mouse glider, a rubber spider, and a sticker book. Then I played again and traded everything except the glider (I'd gotten three more smalls) for a little pink rabbit. I also played a game where three balls must be thrown into a muffin tin. Each hole has a number in it. Add up the numbers from each hole your balls fell into. If the sum is under 8 or over 12 you get a stuffed animal. The first time I won a big blue rabbit. The second time I got the number 9 so I didn't win anything.

After that we walked through the rides. They weren't very good so I didn't go on them!

When we were done with Funland, we passed the livestock barns. Daddy and Kara stopped there while the rest of us went on to the big slide. The slide must have been at least 60 feet high and it has several big bumps in it that we had to go over. It was lots of fun! I went down the slide twice and then went to the handicraft corner.

There they had many different kinds of embroidery. We didn't stay very long. As soon as we left we saw the merry-go-

Occasional Owatonnan

First Edition
409 E. Main, Owatonna, MN 55060 Nov. 1990

Editor: Tammy Allen
Reporters: Mr. and Mrs. Allen and Kent

Gifts From Heaven
by Kent Allen

Mountains,
Gifts from Heaven,
Rise on the horizon,
Provide snow,
   skiing, scenery,
And life.

Happy Thanksgiving!

"Over the river and through the woods to Grandmother's house we go..." Thanksgiving '90 finds our family traveling the two and a half hour trip to Westbrook, Minnesota, to celebrate the holiday with Grandpa, Grandma, the Don Odens family, and the Paul Odens family. What fun, food, and sharing we anticipate! By the time most of you receive this newsletter, Thanksgiving will be past, but as we write it, we are looking forward to the time together with relatives.

We hope your Thanksgiving and Christmas seasons are filled with praise to God who has blessed us by loving us and providing the way for us to be righteous in His sight through His Son Jesus.

================================

A Family Poem

We celebrate Thanksgiving Day
  With food and friends and prayer.
We will be glad to hear you say
  That we are welcome there.
The thanks we give is to our God
  For blessing through the year
So let us gather round the food
  And give our Lord a cheer!

(A group effort by Tammy, Kent, Mom and Dad Allen.)

================================

Write Personal Biographies

Every family has its stories that are resurrected and shared at holiday gatherings, often to the embarrassment of the subject of the story. Rachel shared such an incident with her college writing class, telling about the time her father grabbed his shotgun to deal with a rat he had spotted in the basement. After a mighty explosion he returned to the living room with a mutilated bedroom slipper in his hand and a sheepish look on his face.

But how many of those stories have been lost over the years because no one in the family took the time to write them down? Do you even remember the events that occurred on the days that marked the big events in your life? Peter Stillman encourages parents to write an account for each child about the events that took place the day he was born. We thought it was a great idea until we actually tried to remember those events. How we wished we had kept a detailed record of everything that happened on those four important days of our lives!

One of the greatest gifts I have ever received from my father is a one-hundred-page self-published book called *Still Climbing*. One of the first tasks he set for himself after retirement was recording his own personal history for the enrichment and benefit of his children and grandchildren.

> Arthur William Allen was born on Monday, April 6, 1914. This was the year when World War I started. He was born to devoted Christian parents, William Alonzo and Ethel Pamelia Allen. Arthur does not remember April 6, 1914, for his memory only goes back to November 11, 1917, Armistice Day. He remembers his Aunt Ora answering the "general ring" on the old crank telephone hanging on the wall. She turned with a tear in her eye and said, "The war is over." Before the days of radio, the way to spread the news was with the telephone operator in town giving a long "general ring" over the country lines. The second the ringing stopped every woman would rush to take down the receiver and listen. This time it was good news. The war was over.

Most of the accounts in *Still Climbing* would be of interest only to the family, like the fact that although Dad was named Arthur by his parents, the blind doctor who delivered him forgot his name and recorded it as John with the county clerk. But the stories he included can also suggest ideas for the type of memories your children and grandchildren will treasure. My brother and sisters and I particularly enjoy his account of how he met our mother, Verna Allen.

It was at the Richard's Treat Cafeteria a little blond girl caught his eye. Verna Josephs was the manager of the food shop in the same establishment. She was invited to a Bible study attended by more than twenty employees of the cafeteria. Arthur taught the class. Verna was invited by her brother Lester to the Central Baptist Church in St. Paul and it was there she accepted the Lord as her personal Savior.

Since Dad has guided over twenty-five Bible Lands Tours, the account of his first trip abroad was of great interest.

In 1948 Rev. Allen was sent to Beatenberg, Switzerland, as the youth-rally representative from Montana. From there he went to Greece for youth meetings and church services. Lt. Creston Cathcart of the U.S. Navy arranged a Sunday service in which some eighty commissioned officers were in attendance when Pastor Allen preached the gospel of salvation and told them how to be saved.

The only disappointment on that trip was the refusal of our State Department to let him visit Palestine. It was the year that Israel won the War of Independence and was named the State of Israel. It was not considered safe for civilians at that time.

The pace of discovery in this century becomes vivid when we read the account of what transportation was like when Dad was a boy.

From a horse-drawn school bus to flying over six hundred miles an hour has been the experience of that boy born on an Iowa farm. When Arthur first started to school, the horse-drawn school bus stopped each morning at the mailbox to pick up him and his sister Lillian. In 1917 Dad Allen purchased a brand new 1917 Model T touring car. Side curtains were used when it rained and a heavy blanket kept the passengers warm when fall came. But when real winter arrived, the Model T was placed on blocks, the radiator was drained so the water would not freeze, and there that car stayed until spring. One time Dad Allen drove a reckless 35 mph when he rushed to get Dr. Marsh to attend a severe burn on little sister Margaret.

Roots author Alex Haley says, "When an old person dies without having told his story, it is as though a library burned down." Your children will be thankful if you preserve your library of knowledge for them in written form.

Write a Spiritual Heritage Book

While working my way through seminary, I spent twelve months as part of a janitorial crew whose responsibility it was to clean the Prudential Life Insurance Company building in Minneapolis. The other members of the crew soon learned that my wife and I were both from pastors' families and that we had a total of eight brothers and brothers-in-law who were pastors, Bible college teachers, or Bible college students.

One evening during break, a coworker said, "Bob, could I ask you a question?"

Anticipating some theological puzzler like "Could God create a rock so big He couldn't pick it up?" I agreed.

"When you all get together for Christmas," he said, "who prays?"

It was a good question. I had never given much thought to my spiritual heritage. As I answered, I suddenly realized that being part of a family where everyone knew how to pray was a tremendous heritage indeed.

Several years ago we began the process of collecting testimonies from each member of our extended family for the purpose of producing a "Spiritual Heritage Book" for our children. We wanted them to know how each of their grandparents and all their uncles and aunts came to the moment of spiritual rebirth. We felt it important for them to recognize the ways God has worked in the lives of those who preceded them in our family.

Very quickly we discovered that our spiritual heritage did not begin with our parents. Dad's book, *Still Climbing,* provided this account of early believers on his side of the family:

> Rev. Charles Cross was a Baptist minister who provided for his education by renting his horse and saddle for a little income. It was called bounding out his horse and saddle. This was back in New York state around the year 1800. His son was Captain Edwin Cross who lived only 36 years. Captain Cross was wounded fighting for the North in the Civil War. He recuperated from the injury and gathered together a group of volunteers, marched them to the front, and fought for his country. He was with Company B, 33 Illinois Infantry.

> When Rev. Charles Cross married his son, Edwin, to Pamela Link, he presented them a Bible as a wedding gift. Inside the front cover were the words, "This book will keep you from sin, or sin will keep you from this book." Their marriage was in January, 1861.

My wife's mother, Marie Odens, comes from a line of German Mennonite stock. She provided the following testimony from her grandmother Helena Toews for our spiritual heritage book. It was written down when Grandmother Toews was 91 years old.

> I will try to write down how the Lord has helped and blessed me.

> I was born on June 19th, 1868, in South Russia, Molotchna, in the village of Alexanderthal.

> In 1878 my parents and family immigrated to America. Father, mother, and six children. We arrived at Mountain Lake, Minnesota, on July 6th. Mr. and Mrs. Johann Regier met us. Mrs. Regier was my mother's sister. They took us to their home, that was the home of my grandparents, David Nickels. We stayed with them till my parents bought a farm six miles southeast of Mountain Lake. Here was a sod house, built half-way into the ground. It was alive with bed bugs. After much cleaning we got rid of these unwelcome guests, and we got along for a while.

I was baptized on Pentecost 1888. On October 30, 1888, we had our wedding. We lived that winter with my husband's folks. In March we moved on our own farm five miles northeast of Mountain Lake. There was a barn on the place and we lived in it during the summer months. We built a house and were able to move in before winter.

After we lived on the farm thirty-six years, we decided to move to town. We built a house and moved to town on December 11, 1924.

When Lena became seriously ill this spring, I asked myself, "Will the cup of trials not get too full?" The Lord has helped me to cross this mountain also, so that now I can thank the Lord. He has made all things well. To Him be praise and glory and thanksgiving! He has restored Lena to health again. Marie is happy. He has protected me on my long journey and brought me home safe and healthy.

I read somewhere God keeps no one longer on this earth than till his work is done. I do not know what task He still has for me. I will follow as He leads. I have one prayer, that He will give me faith to the end and a sound mind all of my days. That all my descendants would be saved. God never fails.

We are still waiting for the testimonies of our own children to be written, but when they are, we believe it will be an encouragement if they have before them the lives of other family members who have served God. They will be able to say with the writer of Hebrews, "Wherefore seeing we also are compassed about with so great a cloud of witnesses, let us lay aside every weight, and the sin which doth so easily beset us, and let us run with patience the race that is set before us" (Heb. 12:1).

Write Other Family Memories

The advent of the camcorder has made possible a very simple method of preserving family memories. Weddings, graduations, and even births are now being recorded for future reference. At our last reunion we designated a specific time for Grandfather Odens to tell stories from his childhood, and we captured the entire session on tape.

Cassette tapes can also be used with those who find it more comfortable to talk than to write. Peter Stillman refers to *Family Folklore: Interviewing Guide and Questionnaire,* which offers suggestions to those who plan to conduct such interviews.

They recommend that you ask evocative questions. Let the ones you are interviewing respond with more than just yes and no. Also, be aware that role switching may occur. Even though you are a relative, you have suddenly become a reporter. If this makes your informant uneasy, then try later in a less formal setting with the camera as an observer rather than a participant.

The interviewing guide reminds us of the importance of showing interest. Encourage your informants as much as possible. Interject remarks whenever appropriate. Take an active part in the conversation without dominating it. Learn to be a good listener as well as a good questioner. Remember that older people tire easily; each interview should be a pleasant and rewarding experience for all parties involved.

It is important to know what questions you want to ask, but at the same time don't be afraid to let your informant go off on a tangent. You may learn things you would never have thought to ask about.

An excellent suggestion is to use personal items as memory joggers. Documents, letters, photo albums, scrapbooks, home movies, and other family heirlooms can all be profitably used to stimulate memories.

When you have finished, prepare some sort of written report for the family members as a tangible result of their participation. Remember to save all of your tapes, notes, and any other documentation that you have accumulated. Label everything with names, dates, and places.

This last step may seem tedious, but think about your great-grandchild who, many decades in the future, may be trying to use your oral research to discover his or her own spiritual heritage.

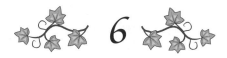

Just the Write Note

Isaac Watts, considered by many to have written the first hymnbook in the English language, composed his first poem when he was only seven years of age. The Watts home was very strict, but one evening during family prayers young Isaac began to laugh aloud. His father stopped reading and called on Isaac for an explanation of this irreverent and unlikely behavior. The boy sheepishly admitted that he had been watching a mouse run up the bell rope and had just made up a rhyme about it.

> A mouse for want of better stairs
> Ran up a rope to say his prayers.

Historians don't record the response of the good deacon and his wife, but in light of the fact that Isaac Watts continued to write poetry, it could be assumed that they encouraged him to do so.

Upon completion of his formal training, Watts returned to the church where his father was a deacon. In those days, the only songs allowed in churches were rather dull, untuneful Psalm-versions read by a clerk and then repeated by the congregation. Isaac wished that the song service could somehow reflect the beauty and grace of God, and one day he complained about it to his father.

"Well, you like to write poetry," his father said. "Why don't you write us some better hymns?" Isaac decided to try it, and the next Sunday he introduced a new hymn, "Behold the Glories of the Lamb." The people enjoyed it so much that he continued to write a song each week for more than two years. By 1707 he had written nearly all the 210 hymns that were printed in the volume *Hymns and Spiritual Songs.*

Writing songs and poems can be a ministry to others when they are shared with family members, relatives, and the church. Since the writing of lyrics for a song and the writing of poetry are similar, we will deal with both of them in this chapter. When one of your family members decides to set his poetry to music, have him record the melody line on tape, then ask a musician to make up a lead sheet, which is a written melody line with words.

The basic principles of lyric writing are the same as for standard poetry: each verse should have the same number of syllables written in the same meter. There are numerous forms of rhyme schemes to use, but one of the basic forms is *abab;* that is, the ending words of the first and third lines rhyme and the last words of the second and fourth lines rhyme. Albert Williams, in the article, "Can You Write Gospel Songs?" says, "The burden of your song goes in the chorus, and don't forget to repeat the title as often as possible."

More important than either meter or rhyme is imagery. "Writing poetry requires a vital interest in words, an instinctive desire to arrange them in original ways, relate a sense of wonder, capture a bit of mystery," says Viola Berg in *Writing to Inspire* (Gentz and Roddy, eds., Cincinnati: Writer's Digest Books, 1982). "Editors are quick to recognize a poem that may have a proper skeleton, even an attractive form, but no pulse."

What mother would not agree that the ideas and sentiment are more important than meter and rhyme in the following poem?

My Mother

My mom is nice,
She does nice things;
I guess I think
She is the best

I love her now;
I always will;
Until she dies;
She'll still be here.

Jeremy Moffitt, age 11

Since ideas in poetry are more important than choice of form, it is an ideal writing medium for children. They will find it easy to imitate the form of other poetry while using their own ideas as inspiration. Don't use the ideas in this chapter to force anyone to write poetry. Instead, use the suggestions as a springboard to catapult your own ideas into the air.

Write Poems

Because poetry often follows a set pattern of rhyme and rhythm, it makes an ideal medium for group composition. The first person establishes the meter and a rhyme pattern by writing the first two lines, and then each individual in the group is invited to follow suit. If you are hard pressed to find two lines to start the process, you can even use lines from someone else's poem. The following group poem was composed by four family members, two adults and two children. See if you can determine which parts were written by each.

A Family Poem
We celebrate Thanksgiving Day
With food and friends and prayer,
We will be glad to hear you say
That we are welcome there.

The thanks we give is to our God
For blessings through the year.
So let us gather round the food
And give your Lord a cheer!

Group efforts at poetry may be initiated in other ways as well. The first person can write a line of poetry, thus establishing the meter. Then the next person can add a line, beginning the line with the last word or words of the previous line. The third person to write should start his line with the last word or words of the second line, and so forth. If the first person were to borrow a line from Joyce Kilmer, "I think that I shall never see a poem lovely as a tree," the next person would begin his line with the "a tree" or "tree." If a large group is playing, once around should be sufficient. Otherwise, write until the poem comes to a logical stopping place. The following poem, beginning with a line from T. S. Eliot's "Preludes," was composed in this fashion by a group of college students.

The winter evening settles down
Down and around the snow swirls,
Swirls around the evening sky
Sky and darkness cover day
Day flees past the time to life
Life is full of surprises.
Surprises bring winter nights to life
Life is not worth living
Unless we give ourselves to Christ.

Christ fills our hearts with peace
Peace and contentment, love and joy
Joy that fills our life with song
Song that makes the ice to melt.

For very young children, parents can write couplets and leave off the last word to help the child develop a sense of rhyme.

We're heading out the door,
We're going to the _____.

I saw a dog
Jump off a _____.

"Rhyming works best when the subject of the poem is not serious," suggests Harvey Wiener in *Any Child Can Write* (New York: Bantam Books, 1990). "Encourage the child to write silly rhymes that play with words in improbable situations."

What Peter Stillman calls "Name Poems" is another poetry writing game that can be played by a group, basing a poem on each person's name. The chosen name is used to provide the beginning letters for each line, and the lines may be one word or several words long. The result will be an acrostic that spells out that person's name. For example, "JENNY" might result in this poem:

Joyful,
Effervescent,
Nice as a birthday present.
Never mean or grouchy
You are sweet as candy.

Marjean Moffitt used a name poem as a gift tag for her oldest boy on his birthday.

Marcus
A Latin word meaning "Defender," a
Reference to a man with strong
Character, one who stands, one who does not waver, one who is
Unique, one who is my
Son!

Write Haiku

A Japanese poetic convention called "haiku" is one of the simplest forms of poetry for the beginner; at the same time, it is a form used by some of the world's best poets. Haiku is usually about one of the seasons of the year. It consists of three lines, the first and third containing five syllables and the second possessing seven. Getting just the right word to fit the pattern gives the poet practice in choosing among similar words. Haiku will often start with a general statement and end with a twist or a surprise.

Seasonal

The frozen ice cap
In summer melts to a pond;
Now we swim and fish.

Kent, age 14

Write Couplets

The couplet is simply a pair of lines that rhyme. Some of the most familiar children's poetry is written in couplets, like Clement Clarke Moore's "A Visit From St. Nicholas."

'Twas the night before Christmas, when all through the house
Not a creature was stirring, not even a mouse.

Harvey Wiener suggests a variety of methods for initiating the writing of couplets. A child may use the words "If I were" to start each couplet.

If I were King David's sling,
I'd teach that old giant a thing.

If I were a manger sheep
I'd give Christ a place to sleep.

"Talk-to-me's" are another idea from Wiener. In this poem the child speaks to an inanimate object, pretending that it can understand.

Mr. Winter, will you please
Stop killing all our trees.
Your cold, sharp, blowing air
Leaves them stripped and bare.
Will you learn that it's not nice
To freeze trees with your ice.
Please take heed of what I say,
Mr. Winter, go away!

Write Limericks

Everyone enjoys limericks and knows how they work. They are five lines long and have a definite meter; they rhyme at the ends of lines 1, 2 and 5, and at the ends of lines 3 and 4. They are fun to write as a group activity or alone and are almost always in a humorous vein. A familiar starting pattern is "There once was—," or "Said the—."

> There once was a man with a cat.
> The cat had been chasing a rat.
> They met with a dog,
> Who was chasing a frog.
> Then the dog started chasing the cat.

Your family will also have fun with limericks by taking familiar ones and supplying a new final line of their own. Try your hand at ending this old favorite.

> There once was a lady from Niger
> Who smiled as she rode on a tiger
> They returned from the ride
> With the lady inside
> _____.

Write Riddle Poems

These can be couplets or longer poems, but each must pose a question or riddle for the reader to answer.

What crosses over the river wide
And touches the road on either side?

My name is found in the book of Kings;
I played a harp, among other things.

Write Alliteration

After a child has been introduced to rhyme, it would be helpful for him to learn about other types of sound-effect language. One that will add to his enjoyment of writing couplets is alliteration, the repetition of beginning sounds. To begin, you may want to make up lists, for example, of words that begin with the sound of *j* or *a* or *t*.

Jim	apple	top
jacks	animal	tumble
jump rope	agile	torpedo
gymnasium	ant	tiny
jerk	add	toad

After the lists are finished, encourage your child to write the first line of a couplet, using as much alliteration as possible. Tell him not to worry about making sense. Nonsense rhymes are an excellent way to learn about language. He may write:

The tiny toad tumbled from the torpedo top.

For the second part of his couplet, have him write another nonsense line, ending it with a word that rhymes. He might finish it this way:

The sailor in the swimsuit screamed, "Stop!"

Another child may choose to make a rhyming and alliterative couplet with the "a" words; another with the "j" words, and so forth.

Write Sensory Images

Anything children enjoy doing may be used as the theme of a poem. Activities like sledding, singing, reading, swimming, skiing, fishing, hunting, racing, or skating provide stimulation for sensory images. Touch, taste, smell, sight, and sound are important in poetry because most often it is our senses that trigger an emotional response.

Animals are favorite subjects because many children have pets. Pretending to be an animal or imagining an unusual pet may provide a great theme idea for a poem.

> Cats
>
> Cats are silly as bats,
> They chew on there hats.
> They look for a mouse,
> In a big house.
> They run from bares,
> And sit on chairs.
>
> Kelsey Williams
> and Wendy Allen,
> age 8

Harvey Wiener suggests starting poems with colors and objects that share a common visual characteristic. Begin a poem by giving the child a question such as "What is yellow?" Let him think about something with that color and then write the next line, "The sun is yellow." To finish off the three-line poem, follow Wiener's suggestion: "The child expands upon the idea he just expressed, offers details of setting, action, or place, and rhymes with the color word at the end of the line."

What is yellow?
The sun is yellow.
Just like my jello.

The same approach may be used for each of the senses. Give the child a question involving sound, smell, taste, or touch, and have him answer the question and then expand on the answer with a rhyme. Here are four such questions to start with. You will enjoy adding your own.

What goes moo?
What smells good to eat?
What is sweet?
What feels rough?

Family members can also make collections of words that describe sounds, smells, tastes, and the way things feel.

ring-a-ling	smooth	warm	sharp
ding-dong	prickly	frigid	dull
buzz	glassy	sweet	fresh
boom	jagged	sour	stink

Encourage your young writer to use a sensory word in each line of his poem.

Write Similes

Because they follow an easily identifiable form, similes are a good place to begin when introducing children to figurative language. Explain that a simile uses "like" or "as" or some such expression to compare two objects. Then your family can make a game of seeing who can find the most similes in familiar poems or in Scripture verses as you read them aloud.

> And he shall be like a tree planted by the rivers of water, that bringeth forth his fruit in his season; his leaf also shall not wither; and whatsoever he doeth shall prosper. The ungodly are not so; but are like the chaff which the wind driveth away. (Ps. 1:3-4)

As the hart panteth after the water brooks, so panteth my soul after thee, O God. (Ps. 42:1)

As snow in summer, and as rain in harvest, so honour is not seemly for a fool. . . . As coals are to burning coals, and wood to fire; so is a contentious man to kindle strife. (Prov. 26:1, 21)

Once your child is familiar with the form of the simile, provide an opening line and challenge him to think of as many comparisons as he can. Try to provide many opportunities for him to use his senses.

My dog sounds like . . .

Our back yard smells like . . .

My room is as clean as . . .

God's hugs are like . . .

James Smith, in *Creative Teaching of the Language Arts in the Elementary School* (Boston: Allyn and Bacon, 1973), tells of a boy named Billy who in the third grade "took 'sweet as a rose' and turned it into 'sweet as peppermint fudge.' When the teacher said, 'Well, that's good, but I never had peppermint fudge,' Billy responded, 'Well, neither did I, but I bet it's mighty sweet.' " Smith ends the story by saying, "Billy is a scientist!"

Write Cinquains

Another simple form of poetry that is fun for family activities is the cinquain. Cinquains consist of five lines. The first line has one word, the second line has two words, the third has three, the fourth four, and the fifth line returns to one word again. The lines don't need to rhyme and any meter can be used. The idea of the poem is what matters most.

Cinquains lend themselves well to group writing. Have each person write one line, and then the last writer can tie the thought of the entire poem together with a one-word bow.

Vacation

Summer
Time to
Play with friends.
Swimming, biking, hiking, having
Fun.

Write Songs

Isaac Watts performed a great service to the church by writing such songs as "When I Survey the Wondrous Cross" and "Joy to the World." The opportunity to serve others through the poetry and songs written by a family is even greater today.

The Frumious Bandersnatch was written for the deaf ministry at our church; its lyrics and music were a family project. The fun that children can have with words was expressed in one of the songs entitled "Word Games."

Have you ever been walking and seen a boardwalk?
Have you ever watched the butterfly?
Can you think of a word that rhymes with *talk,*
Yet silently soars high in the sky?

If an elephant married a bluebird,
Could Bluephants or Elebirds sing?
If a spring fell into a spring in the fall,
Would the spring fall up in the spring?

While the children attended a small Christian school in Montana, we offered to write a script and a group of songs for a school program called "His Story." The script called for a group of detectives to search out the mysteries in the eleventh chapter of the book of Hebrews.

We're searching it out, trying to find,
  Good things to put in our mind.
Reviewing the clues, the true and the best.
  Detectives of His Story—That is our quest!

The detectives followed up a missing persons report, the story of Enoch. They investigated a murder, the killing of Abel. And they checked out the story of a grave robbery, the account of Joseph's bones being carried out of Egypt four hundred years after he died. They also listened to witnesses tell their stories of what faith involves.

It's Rain!

Noah: Rain is a-comin', the ark is gonna' ride.
Who'll meet Noah on the other side?
Buildin' is over, hammerin' is still.
Raindrops are fallin' on the window sill.

Townspeople: [*Chorus*] It's rain! (It's rain!)
God has kept His promise (promise).
Rain! (It's rain.)
Fallin' down upon us.
We can't believe what we see, and yet,
Rain! (It's rain!)
We're all wet!

Noah: Animals are settled, God has shut the door.
Who'll meet Noah on the other shore?
Preachin' is over, now it is too late.
All were invited, but we saved just eight.

Noah: Faith is believin', the good old Book is true.
Who'll meet Noah far beyond the blue?
Scoffers are many, followers are few.
God gave His promise, now it's up to you.

By the time they had examined all of the evidence, the detectives had discovered the secret of "Walking by Faith."

> Walking by faith means never seeing
>   But believing anyway.
> Walking by faith means always trusting
>   Though you face a long delay.
>
> Walking by faith means not receiving
>   Without doubting that it's true.
> Walking by faith means calm assurance
>   That God's promise is for you.
>
> Chorus:
>
> They were looking for the Promise
>   They were facing toward the Son.
> They were looking for the Promise
>   Prophets said was sure to come.
> They were looking for the Promise,
>   They were walking in His way.
> They were looking for the Promise
>   Praying, "Savior, come today."

"Christmas in Heaven" was the name of a Christmas drama for which our family wrote the script and the title song. The pastor of a church that used it the first year wrote to tell us what a blessing it was; then he told us of a man who came to his office later that week to accept the Lord. Those are the blessings that will persuade you to continue serving the Lord, His church, your own family, and others through writing.

Write Poetry for Bible Study

Since the purpose of studying the Bible is to see the Word of God become practical in our lives, it is important to apply the Scriptures while studying them. One way to apply them is to write poetry that combines your own emotions and those of the biblical writer. Since the Psalms were originally written in a poetic style and since they deal so often with personal emotions, they lend themselves to such a method of study.

A college student penned the following poems while studying the book of Psalms.

Psalm Six

The grief of this moment is harder to bear
    Until you despair of your life.
The Lord seems to chasten, reprove, and rebuke;
    Every facet is trimmed by His knife.

You plead with Jehovah His mercy to show;
    You ask that His chastening cease;
You long for His kindness, you fondly recall;
    The days when you sought Him in peace.

And now, though it seems that He's turning away,
    Though tragedy makes you grow old,
Remember the shepherd will know that you're gone
    When He counts up the sheep in the fold.

The voice of your weeping the shepherd has heard;
    He's ready to come to your aid.
But now, ask yourself, "Would I be in this mess
    If it wasn't so long since I prayed?"

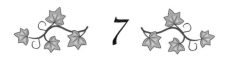

A "Write" Christmas

"As Christmas of 1843 approached, one man could not console himself with such a thought. Again that Christmas, as the director of a London museum and an active man-about-town, Sir Henry Cole had a host of greetings to convey. And it meant writing every one of them by hand," says *A Family Christmas* (New York: Reader's Digest Association, 1984). Henry Cole's solution to his dilemma was to invent the Christmas card. He asked an artist "to portray a scene that depicted his feelings of the season along with a brief message" so that he merely would have to sign his name at the bottom of each card.

The first several years we existed as a family we sent traditional Christmas greetings: commercial cards that said the same things as all the cards we received from everyone else. Soon we decided it was time to put our own mark on Christmas greetings. Using a Christmas tree for a background, we fashioned each member of the family into an ornament and reduced the activities of the entire year to the basics, four words for each of us. The result was the first of many Christmas greetings our family has produced over the years.

The next year we had moved to Colorado and felt that we should include more information than could be contained in four words. Choosing the theme "The Twelve Days of Christmas," we designed a letter that incorporated original drawings to illustrate each event in the song. The text began with this paragraph.

According to the "New York Times" it would cost over $575.00 to send you the gifts of the twelve days of Christmas today. So we have chosen to substitute the following in order to wish you a Merry Christmas from all of us.

From there the letter gave new descriptions for each of the twelve days' gifts. The partridge in a pear tree became the U.S. Postal Service that carried the greeting. Two turtledoves were Carmen and Bob, who celebrate their wedding anniversary on the day after Christmas. Chad, Wendy, and Kent were the three French hens.

"No offense intended, but all of you will do for the four calling birds," was the way the fourth paragraph began. It contained an invitation to keep in touch throughout the year. Five gold rings represented the family of five God had given us. Six geese a-laying equalled the bountiful blessings of God. Seven swans a-swimming posed a reminder to "swim out to see us" now that we were in the West. The "lords, ladies, and maids" of eight, nine, and ten collectively represented the students in the school where we were teaching. Eleven pipers piping announced the arrival of relatives who were coming for Christmas. And the end of the letter spoke of the twelve drummers drumming:

> The story says one drummer boy went to play for the Christ child. Twelve drummers would certainly remind us of the arrival on earth of the Key to all history. "And she brought forth her firstborn son, and wrapped him in swaddling clothes, and laid him in a manger; because there was no room for them in the inn" (Luke 2:7). Have you made room for Him in your inn?

By the next Christmas Tammy had joined the family, giving us the perfect number to fill out all six sides of a Christmas star.

THE CHRISTMAS STAR

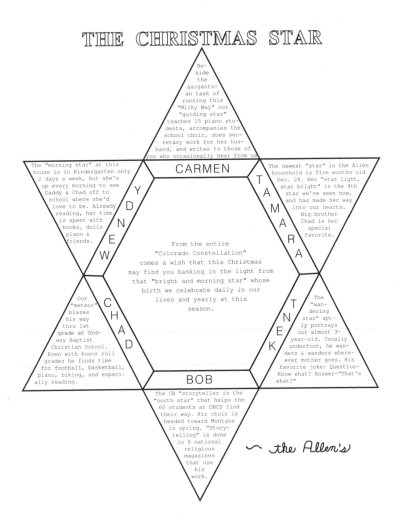

Be-
side
the
gargantu-
an task of
running this
"Milky Way" our
"guiding star"
teaches 15 piano stu-
dents, accompanies the
school choir, does sec-
retary work for her hus-
band, and writes to those of
you who occasionally hear from us

CARMEN

The "morning star" at this
house is in Kindergarten only
2 days a week, but she's
up every morning to see
Daddy & Chad off to
school where she'd
love to be. Already
reading, her time
is spent with
books, dolls
piano &
friends.

DNEW

TAMARA

The newest "star" in the Allen
household is five months old
Dec. 28. Her "star light,
star bright" is the 4th
star we've seen now,
and has made her way
into our hearts.
Big brother
Chad is her
special
favorite.

From the entire
"Colorado Constellation"
comes a wish that this Christmas
may find you basking in the light from
that "bright and morning star" whose
birth we celebrate daily in our
lives and yearly at this
season.

Our
"meteor"
blazes
his way
thru 1st
grade at Ord-
way Baptist
Christian School.
Even with honor roll
grades he finds time
for football, basketball,
piano, biking, and especially reading.

CHAD

TNEK

The
"wan-
dering
star" apt-
ly portrays
our almost 3-
year-old. Usually
underfoot, he wan-
ders & wanders wher-
ever mother goes. His
favorite joke: Question-
Know what? Answer-"That's
what?"

BOB

The CB "storyteller is the
"north star" that helps the
60 students at OBCS find
their way. His choir is
headed toward Montana
in spring. "Story-
telling" is done
in 8 national
religious
magazines
that use
his
work.

~ the Allen's

A family-written poem inside a large bell carried through the theme "I Heard the Bells on Christmas Day." For Thanksgiving that year a friend had shared fractured versions of Christmas carols called "Pumpkin Carols." Singing them had been so much fun that the idea sparked a similar venture for a Christmas greeting. The first and last verses went like this.

I heard the bells on Christmas Day
Send Christmas greetings on their way
From Bob and Carmen, Chad and Kent,
From Tammy Jo and Wendy Rae.

But most of all the bells this day
Their old familiar carols play
Of Christ who came! To all proclaim
His peace on earth, good will to men!

With the theme "Happy Birthday, Dear Jesus" the message was very simple. "The Allens give themselves to Christ this Christmas and invite you to do the same. What God wants most for Christmas is YOU." A birthday cake decorated with a star and manger scene sat in the midst of six presents, one to represent each member of the family.

Another year a simplified version of a family Christmas program provided the text, and the artwork consisted of a curtained stage. Each of the children had a written speech as if he were giving one in a Sunday school program.

PROLOGUE: (Preschool children come to the platform.)

TAMMY: (Age 3. Prompted loudly by her teacher.)
"Christ is born," said the star
Leading wise men from afar.
We can work for Jesus, too.
Shine like stars in all we do.

WELCOME: (Kindergarten children assemble on the platform.)

KENT: (Age 5. Loud and bold without prompting.)
The kindergarten welcomes you to the Allen's home tonight.
We hope our Christmas program will be a real delight.

SONG: (Primary children's choir called "His Kids.")

WENDY: (Age 8)
In school where I love to go,
    I learned songs on the piano.
How God set the stars aglow.
    But best of all, I learned of Christ,
Who died and rose, I know.

RECITATION: (Juniors assemble at the front of the platform.)

CHAD: (Age 10)
My Christmases now number ten. Each one comes so slow and then is gone. But not before I see what Christmas really means to me. It's not the tinsel on the tree or even presents. Nor to me is it the carols or the fire. It's not the stockings, not the treats. What Christmas is—well, here's a clue. He's living all year long, in you.

Going back once again to a Christmas carol for a theme, we found in "Joy to the World" the inspiration for a musical-note greeting. For that Christmas each family member shared a favorite carol and a few quick words about his or her activities of the previous year.

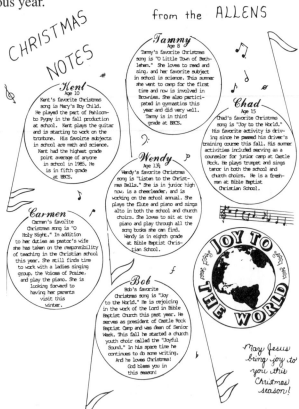

The purchase of a computer and some graphics software gave Kent and Tammy the incentive for designing "Our Christmas Letter (The Sequel)." The dramatic production in three acts used their artwork as a cover.

ALLEN PRODUCTIONS
PRESENTS

"Our Christmas Letter " (The Sequel)

Producer: Robert Allen
Director: Carmen Allen
Starring: Chad, Wendy, Kent
and Tammy Allen

Prologue: Director: We're going to be late with
our Christmas letter again.
Producer: I'll get right on it.

 # CURTAIN RISES

The program itself summarized the year in dramatic terminology, listing the time of action, place of action, and synopsis of each act: spring, summer, and fall. The production concluded with the following epilogue.

> The entire cast and crew joins to wish you a blessed Christmas and a Christ-centered New Year. May Jesus Christ always be the THEME of your life's drama. "But when the fulness of the time was come, God sent forth his Son . . . to redeem them that were under the law, that we might receive the adoption of sons" (Gal. 4:4-5).

Over the years the publication of a Christmas letter has become a family project. Choosing a theme and assigning jobs are responsibilities shouldered by Mom and Dad. Each member of the family gets involved in deciding what should (or shouldn't) be included in the text of the letter, and the one who gets to the computer first gets to do the artwork.

Personalizing your Christmas greetings will help to make the season even more special for you and all who receive your letter. Use the ideas from this chapter or come up with your own. Christmas carols and songs, tree decorations, and your own family traditions should provide you with enough ideas for an entire lifetime of Christmas giving.

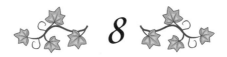

8

The Write Gift

Thousands of young men and women were being called up for military service at the time of the Gulf War, but it didn't really hit hard on the Bible college campus where I was teaching until one of my own students, Tim Fitch, received his orders. Tim was in the reserves, part of the military police, and had been expecting to hear from his company since the beginning of the semester. More than a month of classes still remained, and teachers and students alike rallied around trying to help him finish his work so he wouldn't lose credit.

Tim was enrolled in an oral interpretation course I was teaching that semester. When his classmates heard he was leaving, they planned a farewell party, bought a cake, and then tried to come up with just the right gift to give a young man being pulled away from his college chums to go to a possible desert war halfway around the world.

"I think Mr. Allen should write a poem," suggested Tamera, and I agreed to try. I already knew that sometimes the only way to give the "right" gift is to give the "write" gift.

On the day of the party the class treated Tim to the first oral performance of "The Amazing Tale of M.P. Tim" (with apologies to Robert W. Service). The poem began like this.

There are strange things done in the Saudi sun
By the men who hunt Hussein.
Iraqi trails have their secret tales
Told in words you can't explain.
Iraqi nights have seen strange sights
Full of troops in the shadows dim.
But they ain't seen nothin' until they've seen
The deployment of M.P. Tim.

A gift of writing turned out to be exactly the right gift for Tim. In fact, giving your own writing ranks with cross-stitched throw pillows and homemade goodies as one of the most personalized forms of giving. The gift of writing bears not only the written message but also the unwritten: the giver cares enough to share time, thought, and emotions with the one receiving the gift.

The value of a gift of writing also increases with age. Bev, a college student who is still single, has written a letter describing her feelings on turning 20. Her purpose in writing the letter is to save it as a gift for her own child's twentieth birthday after she marries and starts a family. Such a gift would probably not be valuable to a ten-year-old whose heart is set on the latest doll fashions, but a young lady leaving her teens would find it precious indeed.

For many years our family has compiled "wish lists" to help mom and dad and brothers and sisters choose gifts for one another. One year "Dad's Wish List" included the following item: *One Christmas drama, written and produced by my kids.* What better way to encourage your children to write than to show them that you place a high value on what they produce!

There are numerous ways in which the gift of writing can be packaged. Birthdays, Christmas, Valentine's Day, Thanksgiving, Mother's and Father's Days and all of those special occasions like "Un-birthdays" and "The monthly anniversary of the first time you talked to me" can be celebrated with the gift of writing.

Give Poetry

One of the traditions at the Allen house is called the "twenty-four days of Christmas." Our wedding anniversary is the day after Christmas; so the two celebrations were already intertwined, and I began giving a small gift to my wife Carmen, or "Carm" as we often call her, each day in December leading up to those two big days. Giving that many gifts required some ingenuity since finances were often tight during that time of the year. One answer was for many gifts to be gifts of writing.

After several years of following this tradition, Carmen had nearly a book-size manuscript of poetry; so one year I prepared wooden covers using wood-burning tools to inscribe the title *Untold Tales*. Between these covers I bound copies of all my gift poems to her.

If your poetry is like mine, the only way anyone will ever own it is if you give it away. But those who receive it will treasure it simply because of the source and the emotion it engenders. Most of the *Untold Tales* will remain forever untold, but one sample should encourage those who think they can't write poetry to give it a try.

Word Perfect

Moses composed on papyrus
    Using betel nut juice for his ink.
David wrote psalms on a sheepskin,
    Quite right for a shepherd, I think.

Amos wrote sayings on pottery shards,
    Etching the words with a knife.
Amanuensi did all of Paul's work,
    Since he couldn't dictate to a wife.

Ink was derived from the cuttlefish pouch.
    Cicero used it to write.
Paper was still not available yet
    'Til Ts'ai Lun got the recipe right.

A thousand years later, in China again,
  Pi Sheng made clay movable type.
Then Gutenberg printed a Bible
  Unleashing a torrent of publishing hype.

This poem's typed by computer,
  But don't let the change cause alarm.
I know this machine's "user friendly."
  "Word perfect" can only mean "Carm."

We have several self-published poetry books that have been given to us by friends. Graphics programs for computers have made simple publishing techniques available to many. Robin Adams stopped in just before she left college for Christmas vacation to leave a copy of her book called *In God's Hands*. Wavie Charlton, a dear friend in her eighties, and her brother Clarence Jones have shared several such books with us over the years.

Give a Personalized Story

Since the family generation of our children contains twenty-six first cousins, the question of what to give for birthdays and Christmas has always presented something of a problem. After seeing an advertisement for a "personalized" Christmas story, and being the proud owners of a new computer, we decided that each of the cousins would receive a story in which he or she would star.

The first step was writing the story, taking care to write it in such a way that it could be adapted for families with one to four children. We came up with the title "The Allens Rescue the Christmas Angel," planning to replace our names with those of the other families as we made personalized copies. It was a simple story—a little angel who was supposed to join the heavenly chorus above the shepherd's field gets lost in time and shows up at the Allen home by mistake. The children discover her perched on top of their tree, crying over her terrible mistake. Since they don't know how to travel through time they suggest that the angel fly over to the manger scene in front of their church to sing for Jesus there. Excited that the Christ child has already been born, the angel disappears, leaving only her twinkle behind on the top of their tree.

After writing the story we entered it into the computer along with the names of the cousins from all ten of our brothers' and sisters' families. Soon we had original print-outs of each story, personalized for Ethan, Emily, Eric, Elise, Marcus, Scott, Jeremy, Andrew, Sarah, and all the rest of the cousins. Mother contributed original artwork, the children colored each illustration, and with simple cardstock covers, the books were on their way.

The next year we decided to follow up with a new twist. This time, instead of personalizing the story for each of the cousins, we wrote a story that was incomplete. Spaces were available for each child who received the book to write in his or her own name, address, favorite food, and numerous other items of information as the story progressed.

When the story was complete, we again printed multiple copies using the computer and prepared them for distribution to the cousins. The same type of gift could have been purchased at a toy or book shop, but this was the "write" gift for them.

Give Paste-up Books

Not every writing gift you give needs to be completely original. Children will enjoy cutting words and letters out of magazines and pasting them together to form messages. This method can be used for the construction of homemade Valentine cards, birthday cards, or party invitations. It is also an easy way to put together rebuses, in which pictures take the place of certain words.

Another variation of the paste-up book is to mount a picture on a blank piece of paper and then write a new caption or cartoon-style balloon conversations for the people in the picture. For a fortieth birthday celebration, Marcus, Scott, and Jeremy compiled large pictures of the pyramids, a redwood, and the sun and labeled them all as "things older than Dad."

Give Drama

Making Christmas more than a day of new toys, tinsel, and turkey has always been a concern in our family. Gift giving is exciting, and sharing a holiday meal with the family is memorable, but we continually sought for ways to turn our minds toward Christ, the reason for our celebration.

When my wife's grandfather was still alive, family tradition required every child to stand in front of him and recite his or her lines learned for the church Christmas program. Then Grandpa Toews would pull them close in a bear hug and squeeze a dime into their fist.

Our children were still quite small when they lost their great-grandfather, so new traditions were needed. Family Christmas dramas became a part of our post-Christmas dinner activity.

One of the first of these dramas was presented when several of the cousins were too small to talk. It was decided that they would be sheep with paper bag masks. The older children portrayed the other animals who observed the birth of Christ in the stable. In their drama the animals were arguing over who should be allowed to sleep in the manger, and each one had a reason why he should be given the privilege. Then Mary came with the Christ child, and each animal in turn recognized that He was the one who should be given the place of privilege in the manger.

From these early Christmas dramas came the idea for more structured plays when the family assembled for periodic summer reunions. Written by one member of the family and performed by all the cousins at the end of the week-long reunions, they have become a highlight of the event. The plays have ranged from a take-off on familiar children's literature called "Take That, You Villain TV" to a full-length spoof of mystery plays called "The House of Agatha Mystrie."

The problem of including all the cousins in the play has been solved in various ways over the years. In "Take That, You Villain TV" two preschoolers were called from the audience to help defeat the villain, and they didn't have to learn any lines at all. One production, "The Animated, Illustrated, Musical History of Israel" used two narrators, with all the rest of the cousins participating as a mime troupe.

Not only did the writing of the plays become a gift to the family, it provided a means by which all the grandchildren could participate in giving a wonderful evening of entertainment to their parents and grandparents.

Give a Signature

One of the easiest gifts to give is your signature. Everyone loves a signature on the bottom of a check for $25.00, but there are other signatures that can be just as greatly appreciated.

Mother's tablecloth began as a wedding present, a plain, white cloth that, as the best she owned, was saved for special occasions. It would have remained a plain, white tablecloth if it hadn't been for Paul Pretiz.

Paul was a musician who accompanied an evangelist on a visit to Dad's first church in Baker, Montana. While waiting for the coffee after dinner, Dad asked him to sign a guest book, and without waiting for the book to appear, Paul pulled out a big fountain pen and proceeded to autograph Mother's clean white tablecloth in indelible black ink. Mother arrived from the kitchen just in time to see him add an octave of piano keyboard to identify his occupation.

We had to admire mother. You would have thought she had people autograph her tablecloth every day. And from that day on, she did. Finances wouldn't allow another tablecloth so Mom went to work with decorating pens and added color to the keyboard. After that, all guests were asked to autograph the tablecloth, in pencil, and Mother would fill in the signature with color.

Many interesting names were added to Mother's tablecloth, each one carrying a special memory, and every time it appeared we would go over the names, remembering the times we enjoyed with the guests and wondering who would be next. It actually became a written reminder of the godly people who came through our home as we grew up.

You may not want to turn a tablecloth into a scratch pad, but the front or back cover of a Bible is an excellent place to collect signatures and the favorite verse references of visiting church speakers. A guest book at your front door will help to remind your family of the fellowship times you shared with others. A commercially produced autograph book is an inexpensive gift for children that will start them on an interesting hobby that could one day prove valuable as well.

Give Other Gifts of Writing

Once your family determines that writings are of great value both to the giver and the receiver, they will think of many other gifts that can be given. Jeannie Moffitt, one of my wife's sisters, has taken calligraphy classes and prepares beautiful framed prints as gifts.

Notes that promise gifts to come are also welcome as presents. An entire booklet could be prepared with such entries as the following:

For Mother:
An entire day without doing any dishes.

From Tammy

For Mother:
I promise to make my bed for a whole week without being told.

Chad

For Mother,
A day of shopping with lunch at McDonalds.
I'll pay.
                    From Wendy

For Mother
A hug and a kiss. (but only one.)
                    From Kent

Posters, signs, and plaques; cartoon strips, stories, and poems; skits, monologues, jokes, and riddles; histories and biographies; songs and maps—anything that can be written may be given as a gift. And don't forget tools that make excellent gifts for writers: pens and pencils; desk lamps and typewriter ribbons; computer paper, blank disks, or even a computer. Get started writing and you'll never be at a loss for just the "write" gift.

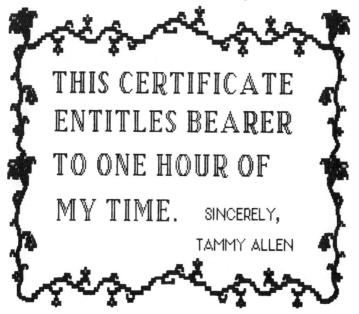

THIS CERTIFICATE
ENTITLES BEARER
TO ONE HOUR OF
MY TIME. SINCERELY,
         TAMMY ALLEN

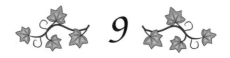

Serving Write Handed

We were all nervous. Guards had inspected both us and our luggage closely before admitting us to the waiting room. Royal Jordanian Airline personnel were stationed at every door, refusing entrance to any who lacked proper documents. Tensions ran high in the Middle East during the summer of 1990. Rock throwing incidents on the West Bank, airplane bombings in Europe, and the threats of Saddam Hussein in Iraq had a stark immediacy for a group of Americans preparing to board an Arab airliner for a flight to Amman, Jordan.

Seating was at a premium as enough passengers to fill a 747 jumbo jet jostled for some vestige of waiting comfort. Across the aisle, a man with thinning hair engaged a young Arab student in conversation. The boy was returning to his home in Kuwait after a year of college in New York State. As I watched, the man pulled a piece of paper from the inside pocket of his suit coat and handed it to his companion. I didn't have to eavesdrop to hear what they were saying.

"Would you like something to read while you wait?" asked the older gentleman. "It's a short pamphlet I wrote myself."

"A passport?" The Kuwaiti read the cover.

"That's what I call it. It's a passport for the last trip I intend to take."

"Do you travel often?"

For the next half hour the conversation continued as the student read the gospel tract and his companion fielded questions that ranged from why he was going to Jordan to how he could be certain that heaven was his final destination. Several hours later as we prepared to board our airliner, people up and down the line carried not only their own passport but a gospel passport as well.

The man with the thinning hair was my father. He has made it a practice for many years to use gospel tracts that he has written himself. Since he does his own printing, they are not in full color like many other tracts, but they have an advantage over those slick pamphlets. "I've never had anyone turn me down when I offer them something I have written myself," he says.

There are many types of witnessing that can be accomplished through writing or that can be encouraged by the written word. Christ felt that it was important not only to deliver His message orally but also to see that it was written down for others to read. "Ye shall be witnesses unto me," He told His disciples, and we have the same message today because Luke wrote it down. Using writing as a means of witness is an excellent way to involve your entire family in the vital task of communicating the good news of salvation.

Write Gospel Tracts

The passport tract that my father shared with the man on the airplane compares the requirements for unrestricted travel in this world to those for the world to come. Just as a person must show a birth certificate in order to obtain a passport for travel abroad, a person must experience the new birth through Jesus Christ in order to travel to heaven. Just as you cannot obtain a passport for someone else, you cannot obtain salvation for someone else. Comparisons between the international travel and the spiritual journey are used throughout the entire pamphlet.

Comparison is an easy method to use in writing your own gospel tract. Christ often used this method when He taught by means of parables. He compared salvation to finding a lost coin, the growth of a seed, the rescue of a straying lamb, the return of a wayward son, and the discovery of a great treasure.

Nathaniel Olson mentions tracts in *The Successful Writers and Editors Guidebook* (Walker, Franzen, and Kidd, eds. Carol Stream, Ill.: Creation House, 1977). He says that an excellent method for writing tracts is to "get a new slant on an old subject." He recommends using words, expressions, or illustrations that are your own, instead of imitating somebody else.

Maybe your family has planned a trip to Disney World. You could start with that experience and compare it to planning a trip to heaven. A family member's favorite hunting or fishing story could be compared to various methods of sharing the gospel. God's way of salvation could be compared to a recipe, blueprints for a new house, or a plan for the building of a tree house.

You might want to spend one month during your family worship time writing gospel tracts. Have each member of the family select a personal or family experience that by comparison illustrates a spiritual truth. Younger children might remember a time when they were separated from parents at a fair or in a large department store. Then they could compare being found by parents and being sought and found by God the Father. Teen-agers could describe someone who was disqualified from winning a race because he broke the rules and then compare it to the importance of meeting God's requirements for eternal life.

Christ used some of the most commonplace events of life to illustrate truth—activities like cleaning a house in search of a lost coin. If each family member writes from his own experience, he will end up with a short presentation of the gospel that has a unique appeal because it is personal.

Another method of preparing a gospel tract is for a child to share his own salvation experience. He may not think that the circumstances surrounding his salvation are very exciting, but people who know him will find it interesting.

A family member's testimony could be given in two different ways, depending on when it was he met the Lord. The first is the chronological approach, used by those who were converted later in life. For this approach, he should tell his life's story in a conversational manner, leading up to the time of his salvation. He could show how God used His Word and the places, people, and circumstances of his life to bring him to faith in Christ.

The second approach is called the overview or flashback approach. If a person came to Christ at an early age or feels that his adult life has been more interesting than his early life, he could try this method. The idea here is for him to give a general overview of his life up to the present time. Then he can flash back to the spiritual turning point in his life, making the transition with a statement such as "Let me share with you the greatest event that has happened in my life."

When we worked on this project, my wife decided to use the second method.

> May I share with you the greatest event that has happened in my life? I grew up as the middle child in a family of seven children. We were pretty normal, except that we were also "pastor's kids." I was exposed to all the activities of older siblings and younger ones. After growing up in southern Minnesota, I graduated from high school and went to Bible college, where I met my husband.
>
> The event that changed the focus of my life happened when I was in elementary school. At that time I realized that I would never be as good as God wanted me to be, and I could not be holy like He is.
>
> I had often heard about Jesus Christ coming to earth, but at that time I realized why He came. It was because He loved me and was willing to pay the price of God's judgment for my offenses against His holiness.

It was pretty special to realize that Jesus, God's Son, loved me (and each person in the world) and was willing to provide this way for me to become acceptable to God. When I understood what Jesus had done for me, I prayed and accepted what He did for me as the way that I could become right in God's eyes.

That event has had an effect on all the rest of my life. My purpose in life now is to make sure other people know that they can have this same relationship with God—they don't have to be afraid of God's punishment if they pray, accepting that Jesus Christ also provided for them to be right before God.

That's why I want to share this with you. Have you had this happen in your life?

In both of these methods it is important to use informal vocabulary, avoiding religious words or jargon. The Christian world has developed a vocabulary that often means little to the unsaved mind. Instead of talking about "going forward," for example, you could say, "I decided to turn my life over to God."

Try writing out your testimony in five hundred words or less. Then type it up in the format of a tract, make several copies and give them out prayerfully.

Correspond with Pen Pals

On the same trip to Israel, our tour group stopped to visit a missionary in Austria by the name of Martha Yongewaard. We crowded into a small room in the hotel and listened as she shared her testimony. She had been serving in Austria for more than twenty years and had arrived there as a direct result of writing.

When Martha was a young girl she wanted a pen pal, and finally she began writing to a girl who lived in Austria. Letters were exchanged, a friendship blossomed, and out of that friendship a desire grew in Martha's heart to reach her friend for Christ. After several years of corresponding, Martha visited her pen pal, and during that visit God impressed on her the spiritual needs of many others in the land of Austria. Her pen pal has not yet placed her faith in Christ, but she and many others have been the recipients of

Martha's faithful witness over the years. Today there are many in Austria who do know the Lord because one young girl decided to share her faith through the mail.

Pen pals can be contacted through a variety of sources. If your child already has a pen pal, encourage him to witness to that individual by writing in his own words what Christ has done for him. Asking questions about the religious customs of a pen pal can be a means of learning about religious practices in other countries. That will help your child understand the spiritual needs around the world and will enable a witness to grow naturally from his correspondence.

One of your children might want to establish a friendship with an international student studying in your hometown; then they could become pen pals after the student returns home. Many Christian families have opened their homes to foreign exchange students and participated in a ministry of helpful service that has made possible opportunities to witness. A Christian high school student could also participate in the exchange program by living abroad for a term, thus making friends with whom the gospel could be shared.

Any of your family members that travel could begin a correspondence with people they meet; this is a good way to extend a casual contact for the glory of God. One man who travels often to the Middle East placed an advertisement in the *Jerusalem Post* offering to exchange Montana agates for semi-precious stones from Israel. The contacts gained allowed him to visit in several Israeli homes and give them not only Montana agates but also a word concerning their "cornerstone," the Messiah Christ Jesus.

Children can be encouraged to correspond with other children whose parents are missionaries. One Christian writer shared how her parents kept a world map on the wall of their breakfast room. Each member of the family was challenged to have a heart for the entire world. They wrote to their missionaries and found out what their particular ministries were. For some it was teaching school or practicing medicine; others specialized in evangelism or church planting. In this way her family members kept abreast of the specific needs of missionary families. They also asked them to send regular prayer letters or newsletters.

For several years our family had a "foreign night" once each month. My wife would cook a meal with a definite foreign flavor—curried chicken from a Sri Lanka recipe or the great favorite, Mexican tacos. Sometimes we would wear costumes, give reports on customs, or sing a song from that part of the world. But we always included a missionary letter.

The National Council of Teachers of English, in a pamphlet titled "How to Help Your Child Become a Better Writer," suggests that families "share letters from friends and relatives." They recommend that you "treat such letters as special events." What better way to impress upon your children the importance of world missions than to treat letters from missionaries as special events!

Those who are serving on the mission field can include their children in their ministry by encouraging them to write too. The Brammer children, serving with their family in Taiwan, send a newsletter out to other children their own age in supporting churches. The letter gives them an opportunity to take an active part in the work their parents are doing for God. And it is a means of ministering to young people, challenging them to dedicate their lives to a cross-cultural ministry.

Check with your church office to find a missionary family that has children about the same age as those in your family. Then make it a family project to correspond with that family. Clip articles concerning the World Series and the Superbowl and enclose them with your letter. American sporting events receive little coverage in foreign newspapers. American church news receives even less. Besides sending sports and local church news, keep your missionary informed on what is happening in your denomination and in the church at large.

Ask your chosen missionary family whether the children collect stamps or baseball cards or coins; then offer to exchange with them. Share vacation, school or youth group experiences and ask them to do the same. Cut your favorite cartoons out of the newspaper and enclose them with your letter. It may be the only way your pen pal will ever meet Garfield or the strange characters of "The Far Side."

Mom, offer to exchange recipes. Send church news concerning ladies' programs, weddings, and music specials. Share news about clothing styles and colors. Jacki Niefeldt, in a workshop session at a state meeting in Minnesota, listed many items that would be of interest to women missionaries. She included in her list things children say and do, a typical day at home or work, success at your church, souls won to Christ, gardening, answers to prayer, trips taken, cartoons and clippings from newspapers and magazines, news concerning other friends of the missionary, names and fields of missionaries visiting the church, and details concerning guild projects and activities such as decorations and refreshments.

Each member of your family can fill individual needs in the lives of your missionary family members by ministering to them through writing.

Write Schoolwork

Many opportunities for sharing a testimony present themselves during the course of a school year. Children in our extended family have had the opportunity to write Christmas programs that included the gospel accounts of the birth of Christ. Assignments in English, history, science and other courses provided excellent outlets for sharing beliefs. One girl wrote her testimony in Spanish for a language class. Another student, when assigned the speech topic "The Greatest Experience I've Ever Had," told of accepting Christ as Savior.

A high schooler active in Montana state high school forensics discovered a unique opportunity for witness by sharing a monologue he wrote about Barabbas. While winning honors in several tournaments, he was able at the same time to share this story about Christ. His presentation started like this.

Alone . . . alone in a prison cell. The door clanks shut, and I am left alone in absolute silence and darkness. Nothing will break the silence, for there is no one to speak. Nothing will split the darkness, for no light could reach this cursed dungeon. I could talk, and talk, and talk, but it would do no good. I could scream, but it would profit me nothing. I could bat out my brains against that stone wall and not a soul would care. There isn't even a rat to keep me company. Only the maddening silence and the horrible, heavy pall of darkness and death.

The conclusion of the dramatic reading showed the effect of Christ's death on Barabbas.

There's the key. I'll kill him. I'll kill this one too. What does it matter? Nothing matters anymore.

What? You're not the guard. John? What are you doing here? How did you get in?

No, don't tease me so. No, John, it can't be true. I'm a condemned man. I die within the hour. I killed a man. I blasphemed God. The high priest has given my soul to the devil. I can't be free. Free?

But how? What? Jesus of Nazareth captured? And condemned? But me, John, how? Of course I know it's the feast day, but why am I released? I'm a murderer. You know that that man has done no wrong.

Free! Saved! He took my place!

Write Thank-You Notes

Mark Twain said, "I can live two months on a good compliment." Too often we limit thank-you notes to Christmas and birthdays, but they are most effective as a tool of ministry when they are offered spontaneously as a result of a blessing received or help given.

After I wrote to a business colleague to thank him for help he had given that went beyond his job description, he stopped me on the sidewalk. "I want you to know that your note is the first one of its kind I have received in fourteen years on this job," he told me. "Thank you for sending it."

You and your family can participate in a ministry of encouragement to others by taking the time to write short notes of thanks. Commercial "thank-you" notes are often quite expensive, but you can easily create your own. Use original children's art work, hand letter the "Thank You," or come up with another way to say thanks.

You Are Appreciated !

Someone in Montana Loves You!

Since you are Too Far Away To Hug!

A good writing project for a child who is taking a computer course would be to design a cover for a family thank-you note.

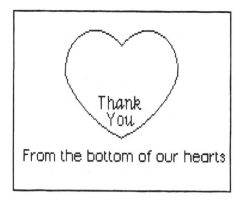

114

Inside the note you should "encourage your youngster to use language that shows his or her unique personality" according to Harvey Wiener in *Any Child Can Write* (New York: Bantam Books, 1990). That is good advice for adults as well. Mention some specific joy resulting from the actions of the person you are thanking.

> Thank you for Sunday's message. The illustration concerning running out of gas really hit home. You helped me get my spiritual tank refilled.

> The encouraging note you wrote on Tammy's poem reminded me of one of my teachers who took time to encourage me in my studies. Thank you for the time you spend teaching our child.

> Thank you for the money you sent on my birthday. I used it when my Sunday School went on a trip to the zoo. I think about you every time I look at the fuzzy stuffed lion I bought.

Maybe writing thank-you notes is one of the chores your children have come to despise. It had become that way for Brian Freerksen when he was ten years old.

"Mom, I think I'll just return this dollar to Grandma," he said as he sat at the dining room table with envelope, paper, and pen in front of him.

"But it was a gift, Brian. Why should you return it?"

"Oh, I don't know." For several more agonizing minutes he stared at the collection of items on the table, then he called into the kitchen again.

"Mom, it's just not worth it."

"What do you mean, Brian? What's not worth it?"

"This." His mother came through the door just in time to see the dollar bill—folded as an airplane—swoop to a crash-landing on the floor. "One dollar is just not worth the effort of writing a thank-you."

Ten-year-old logic did not prevail, however. Instead, his mother taught him that while writing a thank-you may cost something, it is definitely worth the effort. Your children can learn the same lesson.

Writing a thank-you note can be an excellent way to serve Christ. When I was a pastor, my greatest encouragement came in the form of notes from people who took time to write their thanks. Thank-you notes might have been what the writer of Hebrews had in mind when he encouraged church members to "consider one another to provoke unto love and to good works" (10:24). What better means could be used to fulfill that scriptural admonition? Consider how your family can spur others on to love and good deeds by writing your thanks as well.

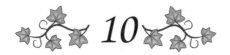

10

The Write to Share

An overflow audience crowded into the university auditorium, and the lights began to dim. A few latecomers scurried to their seats. More and more of the lights faded to black until only one remained. It was a small light that would shine on the face and hands of one lady throughout the entire production. Sue wasn't on stage, but she was a very important part of the production. She was signing the entire musical for the deaf.

Attendance at the play was not the only part that a group of deaf believers was playing, however. *The Frumious Bandersnatch* had been written specifically for them. Their church was presenting it as a fundraiser; the proceeds were designated for the purchase of special equipment to aid deaf students at a Christian school where many of their children attended. The junior high students from the school, along with some university actors, composed the cast.

The Frumious Bandersnatch tells the story of a young girl named Heather. She befriends a deaf girl, Violet, with whom other children will not associate because she can't talk. When the children start to tease Violet, they are chased away from the playground by a huge, blue, furry creature: the Bandersnatch.

When the Bandersnatch asks Heather how she learned to be so kind, she replies with the song, "It's because I met a man called Jesus."

Then the Bandersnatch devises a plan. He takes away the ability of all of the other children to speak, which makes them dependent on Heather and Violet to teach them sign language. They do it with the song "A is A."

A is A, with hands you can portray it,
B is B, no matter how you say it,
C and D, and E and F and G,
All the letters you can make, if you will follow me.

Words are words, but say them with your hand
And words become what everyone can understand
I'll say "hello," "goodbye," and "I love you."
And everyone will know that what we say is really true.

No one but the deaf ministry ever received a dime from the production of *The Frumious Bandersnatch*. The university donated the auditorium, the actors donated their time, and the script and music were written as a ministry.

The "write" to share is a great privilege that can be a blessing to your church, your school, and your family. These ideas for writing to share should in turn generate additional ideas that you and your family can use.

Share Drama

One day I received a letter, along with a short play script, from Barbara, a friend who has taught Sunday school for years. She wanted her class to use drama to present the lesson of Moses and the manna. Failing to find a script that would tell the story and yet fit the abilities of her students, she had decided to write her own.

The story idea in her script was original and significant. But almost immediately after witnessing the birth of that idea she had seen it strangled by problems. Her letter was a plea: "Now I'm writing to say HELP."

Often a teacher finds herself in a situation where available scripts are unusable for her class because of requirements in facilities, or personnel, or both. The solution is to write your own play. The following example, which I shared with that teacher, shows how simple and satisfying it can be to do your own writing. Barbara was asking for the tools that would help nurture her idea until it developed into just the right play for her class.

The first problem she listed involved personnel. Many of the students in her class came from families that gave them little spiritual encouragement. Only two actors would get enough help at home to be able to memorize major parts. Yet she still wanted to include her whole class in the cast.

The answer was to confine the main action of the play to a family. The mother, a part she could play herself, and two sons would carry most of the dialogue. The rest of the class could represent Moses and the children of Israel. These parts would be exciting even without dialogue because of the actions involved. Moses would carry a staff and lead the people and hit the rock. The people of Israel would get to complain, which could be mostly spontaneous, and they would gather the manna and eat it.

The second problem was character development. The action of the story was produced by the hunger the family faced, but every play needs a conflict in order to sustain audience interest. This play needed a conflict within the family.

To produce that conflict, we suggested to Barbara that she make one son, Benjamin, a cooperative child and the other son, Jacob, a complainer. Rewriting each line of dialogue with those personality characteristics in mind made the boys into individuals rather than identical twins. It also produced tension between Jacob and his mother that could be resolved at the end of the play, producing a satisfactory climax.

The third problem was the dialogue. "Dramatic dialogue is not ordinary speech; it is speech concentrated and directed," says Raymond Hull in *How to Write a Play* (Cincinnati: Writer's Digest Books, 1988). The story that the play was to tell was basically outlined by the Scripture, but the actual lines of dialogue needed to do more than tell the story.

Dialogue should be concentrated into three areas: revealing character, creating atmosphere, and advancing the plot. The words spoken by the characters needed to demonstrate the strained relationships, convince the audience that these events were really taking place in the wilderness, and reveal the basic problem they faced—could God meet their need for food? Another rewrite succeeded in accomplishing these three purposes through the dialogue.

The fourth problem strangling the life out of the play was its conclusion. The scriptural conclusion was already evident—God would supply the manna. The conflict in the relationships within the family, however, was still unresolved. The audience was left to wonder whether Jacob ever learned to trust God rather than complain. This was the conflict that would make the lesson practical in the lives of Barbara's students. They would never eat manna in the wilderness, but they would often complain and have to trust God when they couldn't see how He could possibly supply.

In order to provide a satisfactory conclusion, it was important to make the lesson that Jacob learned practical to him. Everyone was hungry and had his need for food satisfied by the manna. In order to make Jacob's lesson practical, we suggested to Barbara that she add two additional complaints to his being hungry. Jacob was upset because he had to gather firewood during the hot wilderness days, and he was complaining because they had run out of honey to put on their bread.

At the climax of the play, when Moses announces that the manna must be gathered, Jacob is still inclined to complain. He figures that this is just another hot job to do, like gathering firewood. But then Moses says that the manna must be gathered early, before the sun melts it. To gather manna, Jacob won't have to be out in the hot sun. Then Benjamin tastes the manna and announces that it tastes like honey. Jacob's other complaint is also nullified, and he realizes that God is concerned about him personally and is able to provide for all of his needs.

With these simple rules in mind, Barbara was able to shape her ideas into a very successful conclusion.

There will be many opportunities for you to write play scripts for your church, school, and home. Just take inventory of the personnel you have available; develop distinctive characters who will grow or change during the course of the play; give them dialogue that reveals character, creates atmosphere, and advances the plot; and devise a strong conflict that, when resolved, will bring the play to a satisfactory climax.

Members of our family have volunteered to write drama scripts for a great variety of situations. Every church is different, and your church would be happy to use a Christmas or Easter program designed specifically with its needs in mind. For a small church in Lake Benton, Minnesota, we wrote a reader's-theater script called "Many Happy Returns." All the children in the Sunday school were involved as shoppers who were returning gifts after Christmas because no one had received the perfect gift. They discovered that the gift they were seeking was Christ.

While living in Missoula, Montana, we wrote a Christmas program script called "A Birthday Party for Jesus." The story itself involved two boys who had received invitations to a party but couldn't find where it was being held. Each class portrayed a different type of Christmas party, and the final one was a birthday party for Jesus, complete with cake.

School teachers will also be happy to see you volunteer an original script for the many programs they present. Thanksgiving, Veteran's Day, President's Day, Valentine's Day, Mother's and Father's Days, and any other holiday can provide the theme for such a program. Bobbie wrote a play as a fourth grader, an account of Washington at Valley Forge, and saw his class present it to their parents at the next Parent-Teacher Association Fellowship.

School program scripts can take a variety of forms. For a school in Ordway, Colorado, we wrote a script that recounted the history of the United States in a way that would tie together a group of patriotic songs the classes had prepared. In Missoula we adapted children's literature, including Dr. Seuss's alphabet book *Big A, Little A,* into a reader's-theater production. For a program at a Christian school we organized a group of detectives called the F.B.I., Faithful Bible Investigators, who investigated several stories from the Old Testament, including the mystery of why Joseph's bones were carried around for four hundred years before they were buried.

Individual students who participate in school or church programs or forensic competitions are often in need of material. While judging a state speech competition for Christian schools, I was surprised to hear one of the contestants using a dramatic monologue I had written more than ten years earlier for a young man in another state. Somehow copies had made the rounds, and the reading, a first-person account of David's fight with Goliath, was proving useful to others as well.

Bible study groups, fellowships, and missionary associations also appreciate drama written specifically for them. When the church ladies from Lake Benton needed a humorous skit to present at a state meeting, we wrote "Patsy," an account of two busybodies who visit the George Washington house in New York to invite the president's wife to join their sewing circle. What the ladies didn't realize was that the woman they assumed to be a maid was actually Martha Washington.

Community drama groups are another group you can serve through writing drama. Follystick Theatre, the children's theater of the Lynchburg, Virginia, city recreation department, wanted to present a history of the city and looked for a volunteer to write the script. I agreed to research the history of the city; as a result I wrote "Seven Hills in Search of a City."

Perhaps your church is looking for a Christmas cantata that would just fit the size of the choir and the style of music your people enjoy. That was the situation when the choir director at our church in Owatonna, Minnesota, suggested that we collaborate on writing our own Christmas drama. After preparing a reader's-theater script for a story called "Christmas in Heaven," we contacted several members of the choir who we thought might be interested in writing songs. The choir director had to add several traditional carols to the program, but the major portion was written entirely by members of the church.

Look around at the groups you would like to serve, contact key people, and make yourself available. Whether you write a monologue, play, skit, pageant, or reader's-theater script, you will discover an exciting ministry in writing to share.

Share Film and Video Scripts

With the advent of the videocassette recorder, more schools and youth groups have begun informal recording of games, programs, and activities. A special project for your group to undertake is the production of a feature-length film on video for presentation at one of the group's functions.

Before camcorders, the only way to accomplish this task was the home-movie camera. One summer in Lake Benton, the Sunday school filmed a program called "The Christmas Spirit of the Shepherds" for presentation at Christmas time. Each class was costumed appropriately as angels or shepherds or kings and transported to Hole-in-the-Mountain Park, where the filming was done with a Super-8 camera. When the film had been developed, it was spliced together into a fifty-minute program. Dialogue and sound effects were recorded; and if the film and recorded sound were started at exactly the same time, everything would be coordinated. The appearance of their children on film drew one of the largest crowds to a Christmas program the church had ever seen.

The problem of coordinating sound and film has been solved by the advent of the video camera. With some careful editing, a satisfactory feature-length film can be produced by a school class, youth group, or family. All they are waiting for is you—to write a script.

Camp is another place where making a film can be a great success. It was at Castle Rock Baptist Camp in Montana that we filmed "The Most Practical Joke of All." The cast was chosen on the first day of senior week so those with speaking parts could start their memorization. The script was written so that the regular events of the camp week figured into the story, making it possible for every camper to be included. By Thursday evening all the filming was complete. Two volunteers stayed up most of the night to do the editing, and on the last day of camp the film was shown for the first time. It later went from church to church to promote the camping season for the following year.

Chad and Wendy both helped to write scripts for a school class and to film them on video. Wendy, along with classmates Mark and Scott, wrote "The Orphan." It concerned a young man who loses both parents in a car accident and has to learn how to be accepted into a new family. Chad's story, "Black Magic Bonanza," was written by Chad, Marc, and Mike. Their film told of a new boy in town who was so desperate to make friends that he tricked other boys into thinking he was Paul Revere. Each film was about thirty minutes long.

In the home, children can make films of favorite stories like "Cinderella" and "Sleeping Beauty." Chad and Kent put together one short feature about a burglar who is detected and captured by the family dog. Children's records can be used to provide narration, sound effects, and music while the story is acted out.

A good way to begin is to have children imitate commercials they have seen on television. Tammy and Kent prepared a spoof of the famous "Where's the beef?" commercial using chocolate chip cookies and asking "Where's the chips?" In addition to commercials, you might want to try capturing the following on your camcorder.

- Play-by-play commentary of favorite games. "And now Sammy moves down the field, controlling the soccer ball as he looks ahead toward the goal. Andy is the only one between him and another score."
- Interviews with Bible characters. "Ladies and Gentlemen, it is my pleasure to introduce to you the winner of

the latest stone and sling competition, David, the giant-killer. David, would you please tell us how you got your nickname?"

- Music recitals. "In all of music history there has never been a duet for tambourine and mouth harp until today. Please welcome Brenda and Bruce with their rendition of 'Oh Susanna' on tambourine and mouth harp."
- Science programs. "Welcome to 'Mild Kingdom,' the science program dedicated to bringing you all of the happenings among the animal and vegetable kingdoms in the back yard of the Allens. Today we will be observing the unusual sleeping habits of Sparky, the family dog."
- Historical events. "This is a great day folks. Today, Henry is driving solo for the first time, and you are there. Watch now as he opens the car door with one fluid motion. He must have practiced that action many times. Now he is in the driver's seat. Will he remember to fasten his seat belt? He does! Listen to that crowd cheer. Gentlemen, start your engines."

Many times it will not even be necessary to write a script in advance for these programs. Appoint a narrator, choose a cameraman, and start those films rolling.

Share Puppet Programs

Mr. Moo arrived at our house just in time for vacation Bible school. The children were excited to have him come along as a visitor, and the rest of the boys and girls at church welcomed him as well. They had never seen a purple cow before.

The scripts we wrote for Mr. Moo, who was actually a purple cow puppet, were very simple. He would listen to announcements and respond with dumb questions that made it possible for the teacher to make the announcement again, thus reinforcing it in the minds of the children. He would try to sing, but instead of singing

"I am a C-H-R-I-S-T-I-A-N," he would sing "I am a C-O-W." Through his mistakes the children learned several new songs.

Soon Mr. Moo and other puppets like him started attending Sunday school and junior church. The children's ministry at our church built a replica of the "Good Ship Gospel" that covered almost the whole side of the gymnasium. For several years my wife, Carmen, wrote the weekly adventures of Pete Parrot, Captain Kid, Handy Octopus, and Toby Turtle as they traveled the world, visiting mission fields.

Puppets are welcome anywhere children gather, and adults enjoy them as well. During a piano recital in which several students were performing selections from "The Nutcracker," Carmen used a puppet to tell the story and introduce each selection.

Children who are hesitant to write stories or even tell them will often find that storytelling with puppets is easy. Place a turtle puppet on a child's hand, and she will begin to create an imaginary world in which that turtle lives. Give another child a parrot puppet and the two puppets will begin to talk, telling a story as they go along. "The best way to learn puppetry is by plunging in and doing it," says Carolyn London in *Puppet Plays for Special Days* (Chicago: Moody Press, 1977). "Don't wait until you have better and more equipment; don't wait until you've learned more; don't wait until— 'Until' may never come."

Share a Radio Program

One of the greatest opportunities for ministry we have enjoyed as a family is the production of the Bible Story Family radio programs. Phil Pantana, the program manager at a Christian radio station in our town, was looking for some original programming; and although we had never tried anything like that before, he was willing to help us make a pilot program. Kent and Tammy hadn't started school yet and couldn't read, so they had to memorize the parts we wrote for them. Chad and Wendy were avid readers and willing to try anything.

Having tried some announcing as a part-time job, I knew what could happen to people in front of a microphone. Phil had given us a one-hour block of time to record a fifteen-minute program. I knew that with flubs and bloopers and retakes we could easily find ourselves at the end of the hour with more program left than we had time.

At the station they grouped the six of us in front of three microphones, Phil started the theme music we had chosen, and we were off. During that first session Mom and Dad had to stop and repeat several lines, but the children were as comfortable in front of the microphones as they were telling stories to each other in the living room at home.

For over a year we continued the weekly broadcast. Each program included a Bible story, retold from a child's point of view, and a contemporary story that illustrated the same point the Bible story was making. We went through the entire fifteenth chapter of the book of Proverbs telling one story based on each verse.

Even if you don't have access to a Christian radio station, you can make story tapes with your family. Take a familiar Bible story, look at it from the point of view of the characters within the story, and write down what they probably would have said. Then assign a family member to each character, read through the script several times, and turn on the recorder.

After moving out to Montana, we took the Bible Story Family programs and reproduced them on cassette tapes that were made available to family and friends for the cost of the blank tapes. My father, who was traveling in Bible conferences, took them along with him and over the next ten years distributed hundreds of them.

When Kent was fifteen and Chad was nineteen, we went hunting in northern Minnesota, stopping on Sunday to visit a church in Virginia, Minnesota. During the service visitors were introduced. When the meeting was over, a family with several small children approached the boys; they wanted to know if they were really Chad and Kent Allen.

"We listen to your stories all the time," said a little girl. "They're the bestest stories I've ever heard."

Somewhere this family had been in a church where my father had been speaking and had purchased a set of Bible Story Family tapes. What a thrill it was for Chad and Kent to realize that they were ministering to a family they had never even met.

Share Family Programs

One of the greatest areas of ministry a family can enjoy is ministering to one another. Family worship, family fellowship, and family entertainment don't just happen; they happen by design. A family that assigns its worship, fellowship, and entertainment to the television, CD player, or even the church will not be as close as the family that develops its own family programs for these areas.

Any occasion can become a time of family celebration. Holidays are natural times to begin, but don't forget birthdays, anniversaries, graduations, wedding showers, and the last day of school.

A family worship time does not have to be elaborate. One Christmas Eve this simple program provided a meaningful experience.

A Christmas Eve Program

Candle Lighting Ceremony................... Tamara
Scripture: Matthew 1:18–2:12 .... Wendy
Solo: "One Small Child" .... Chad
Scripture: Luke 2:1-20 .... Kent
Congregational Song: "Silent Night" .... The Allens

During another holiday season, the children planned an entire evening of entertainment just for their mother. Each of them decided what parts they wanted to play, and then Wendy wrote out a program.

Dancing doll: Wendy Allen
Toy Soldier: Chad Allen
Michanicle bank: Chad Allen
Princess Lee Doll: Wendy Allen
Stuffed Gorilla: Kent Allen
Wind-up puppy: Chad Allen
Rabbit with radio in it: Wendy Allen
Wind-up cat: Kent Allen
Strong man: Chad Allen

At other times a program may come not from a holiday but from the desire to minister to someone who is ill. When Carmen was recovering from an illness, the children made a list of their family-program activities for that day.

1. Plan a treasure hunt.
2. Tell her we love her.
3. Make birthday cards.
4. Presents.
5. Candy.
6. Breakfast in bed.
7. Make a puppet show.
8. Show her that we love her.
9. Do work for her.
10. Read her a story.

Following through on that program resulted in a full day for the family and a very enjoyable recovery period for Mom.

Because of the Bible Story Family tapes, our family has occasionally been invited to minister to churches. By choosing several songs and writing a short narration or skit to introduce each song, we came up with programs such as "The Wonder of It All" and "God Gave a Baby."

You can write a program for your family or church in the same fashion. First, choose several songs on the same theme. Then write a paragraph of narration that tells a story, gives historical background, or explains a situation. Be sure that the end of each paragraph fits the song that is to follow. For a "Western Gospel Night" your script might open like this.

> Narrator: The Old West! Wagon trails, sagebrush, cattle drives and roundups. Custer at the Little Big Horn, Lewis and Clark on the trail to the Pacific, Buffalo Bill Cody, Calamity Jane, and Sitting Bull. The West is all of these and more. But in the midst of the explorers, railroad men, soldiers and gold prospectors were a group of men who stand out as the ones who made the West what it is today. All of the others came and went, but the cowboys came to stay.
>
> Solo: "Christian Cowboy"

Further narration could give historical anecdotes or biographical sketches and introduce such musical numbers as "The Circuit-Riding Preacher" (men's chorus); "The Old Fashioned Meeting" (trio); "The Old Country Church" (quartet); "Just a Closer Walk with Thee" (solo).

Share in Bulletins and Newsletters

The average church bulletin is read about as closely as the small print on the bottom of an insurance form. But it doesn't have to be that way. Volunteer to write for your church bulletin or newsletter and offer a sample of your best writing to those who are in charge. Write short features on missionaries the church supports or on charter members of the church. Make up quizzes, crossword puzzles, and other games. Tell the announcements in story form or in a skit format. Use current events or happenings in your family to illustrate spiritual truth. Here's an example.

> Church was over. Everyone had left the building except three-year-old Wendy who was waiting for her father.

"Daddy, we're alone."

Wishing to reassure her and also provide some spiritual training, I replied, "No, Wendy, we're never alone when Jesus is with us." That seemed to satisfy her.

Upon stepping outside the door, however, she called, "Mommy! Daddy and I are pretending Jesus is with us."

Are you practicing the presence of Christ, or just pretending?

If your church produces a weekly or monthly newsletter, contact the editor and offer your services. Have ready one or two articles of the kind you would like to write, and assure him that you are willing and able to meet deadlines. You could write a humor column; a family-advice column; "how-to" articles for teachers, personal Bible study, the bus ministry, or other church ministries. The possibilities are limited only by your imagination.

Share in the Newspaper

A tremendous outreach program is available to your family through the local newspaper. Although this is not true of large metropolitan papers, smaller daily and weekly papers are often looking for people in the community who are willing to contribute material on a regular basis. Some accept letters to the editor and will publish them on their editorial page. My wife's father, Arthur Odens, has used this means of sharing the gospel in several towns where he has lived. He writes a letter to the editor about a current event, either nationally or locally, and within the letter he shares biblical answers to the problems the world is facing. Usually the newspaper will run the entire letter, including the gospel message.

Other newspapers are looking for correspondents from smaller communities in their reading areas. Write or call to introduce yourself and have something that you have written ready to show them. Bob wrote a weekly high school column for the Billings, Montana, *Gazette* while he was a student at Laurel Senior High School. This opening developed later into an opportunity to write other articles for the paper as well.

If your local paper is hesitant to provide free column space, especially for a religious column, you might approach your church about purchasing the space. Newspaper advertising is still one of the most inexpensive forms of advertising, and in a small community you know that you are reaching into homes your church will not reach in any other way. The key to success in such a venture is to keep the article short and interesting. Give people something they will look forward to reading—something that will grab interest—and share your message as an integral part of the article.

The following article is one of nearly one hundred that appeared in the Lake Benton *Valley News* over the course of several years, inserted as a paid advertisement by our church.

Wet Paint

On the first day of house painting we tried to impress our children with the importance of not touching the wet paint. They did well for several days. Then one afternoon my wife heard the water running in the sink for a long time and went to investigate. There was Chad with a palm full of oil base paint, trying unsuccessfully to scrub it off with soap and water. When she suggested that he wait until Daddy came home so he could clean it off with paint thinner, the reply came quickly, "But I don't want Daddy to know."

Many people apply ineffective remedies to try to rid themselves of sin. They seem to think that if they can somehow get rid of it by themselves, they can keep God from finding out about their sin. But God already knows and has provided the only remedy that will work, the shed blood of His Son Jesus Christ. You must come to him for cleansing. The Bible says, "He that covereth his sins shall not prosper, but whoso confesseth and forsaketh them shall have mercy."

Share a Speaking Choir

One of the exciting new ministries developing in many churches is the speaking choir. A speaking choir consists of a group of individuals committed to sharing Scripture orally in a way that will enhance the meaning of that Scripture for the listener. By dividing the group generally between light and dark voices and then assigning duets, trios, quartets, and other combinations, you can present Scripture in a vivid, exciting fashion.

Speaking choirs have proved successful in camp work. During a music and drama camp held by Castle Rock Baptist Camp in Montana, a group of young people prepared a program that included several Scripture selections; then they traveled to nearby churches to share what they had prepared. Churches have used speaking choirs as an alternative to special music. Youth groups find them a challenging way to memorize Bible passages. School programs and concerts are enhanced by the oral presentation of Scripture. A missionary to Brazil who participated in a speaking choir during his college training has now organized such a group on the field. Church drama teams use the speaking choir as an effective method of introducing plays, focusing the attention of the audience on the biblical theme of the production before the performance begins. Here is an example of how such a choral Scripture reading could be arranged using light (high) and dark (low) voices.

PRAISE
(Psalm 48, Luke 19)

Light duet:	Great is the Lord,
Dark duet:	Great is the Lord,
Light/dark quartet:	and greatly to be praised,
Dark solo:	in the city of our God,
Light solo:	in the mountain of his holiness.
All:	Beautiful for situation, the joy of the whole earth is Mount Zion,
All light:	on the sides of the north,
All dark:	The city of the Great King.
Light solo:	*God* is known in her *palaces;*
Dark solo:	God is known *in* her palaces;
All:	God *is* known in her palaces
All light:	for a refuge
Light duet:	a refuge
Light solo:	refuge.
Dark duet:	And when he was come nigh, even now at the descent of the mount of Olives,
All light:	the whole multitude of the disciples began to rejoice and praise God with a loud voice
All:	for all the mighty works that they had seen:

(The next eight lines should be said simultaneously, like a crowd shouting.)

Dark solo one:	Blessed be the king.

Light solo one:	The king that cometh in the name of the Lord.
Dark solo two:	Peace in heaven.
Light solo two:	Glory in the highest.
Dark solo three:	Blessed be the king of glory.
Light solo three:	Peace in heaven to the king.
Dark solo four:	Glory to the king who comes from God.
Light solo four:	The king cometh bringing peace.
Dark solo:	And when he was come near, he beheld the city and wept over it.
Light solo:	Let Mount Zion rejoice
Light trio:	Let the daughters of Judah be glad.
Light solo one:	Walk about Zion,
Dark solo two:	go round about her,
Light solo two:	tell the towers thereof,
Dark solo three:	mark ye well her bulwarks,
Light solo three:	consider her palaces,
All:	that ye may tell it to the generation following.
Dark solo one:	For this God
Dark trio:	is our God
All light:	for ever and ever;
All:	he will be our guide
Light solo:	even until death?
All:	even until death.

Share Other Writing

The opportunities to use your writing as a means of ministry are all around you. Consider the following list and then ask God to help you and your family find your own means of ministering to others through writing.

- school yearbooks
- company newsletters
- the alumni paper for your alma mater
- reunion booklets compiled by your graduation class
- a cookbook produced by a ladies fellowship group
- school essays and reports
- missionary skits

- stories for Sunday school
- a special birthday program
- a program honoring parents
- narration for a community band concert
- narration for a school choir concert

One of the rewards of helping your children minister to others through writing is the fact that they will begin to minister to you as well. A Father's Day service in church became very special when Kent shared with the entire congregation a testimony he had written concerning his father.

On Valentine's Day while serving at a church in Montana, I received the following note from my nephew.

Dear Uncle Bob,
You encouraged me and a couple days after that I got saved. Thank you, you have been a good pastor! To pastor,
from Andrew

How thankful I was that someone had encouraged him to write that note. How thankful your family will be if you exercise the "write" to share with others.

Writing can, and should be, a serious way in which you share your faith in God. It can, and should be, a way in which your family can serve one another, the unsaved, the church, and the Lord. But don't forget to have fun with writing as well. "To everything there is a season . . . a time to weep, and a time to laugh" (Eccles. 3:1, 4). Since most of us spend more time and effort doing the things we enjoy, enjoying your writing will increase your writing time.

As you share your writing with others and see how it affects their emotional and spiritual lives, your desire to serve others will also increase your writing time. But whether you write to move people's emotions or to tickle their funny bone, the best time to begin is now.

Start writing—"Write" now!

Index